RUSSIA

RUSSIA

Petra Rethmann

ANTHROPOLOGICAL INSIGHTS

UNIVERSITY OF TORONTO PRESS

Library and Archives Canada Cataloguing in Publication
Rethmann, Petra, 1964–, author
 Russia / Petra Rethmann.

(Anthropological insights)
Includes bibliographical references and index.
Issued in print and electronic formats.

ISBN 978-1-4426-3657-6 (softcover).—ISBN 978-1-4426-3658-3 (hardcover).—ISBN 978-1-4426-3659-0 (PDF).—ISBN 978-1-4426-3660-6 (EPUB)

 1. Russia (Federation)–Social life and customs. 2. Russia (Federation)–Civilization. 3. Russians. 4. Ethnology–Russia (Federation). I. Title. II. Series: Anthropological insights

DK510.32.R48 2018   947   C2018-903638-9
                      C2018-903639-7

We welcome comments and suggestions regarding any aspect of our publications—please feel free to contact us at news@utorontopress.com or visit our internet site at utorontopress.com.

North Ameria
5201 Dufferin Street
North York, Ontario, Canada, M3H 5T8

2250 Military Road
Tonawanda, New York, USA, 14150

ORDERS PHONE: 1-800-565-9523
ORDERS FAX: 1-800-221-9985
ORDERS E-MAIL: utpbooks@utpress.utoronto.ca

UK, Ireland, and continental Europe
NBN International
Estover Road, Plymouth, PL6 7PY, UK

ORDERS PHONE: 44 (0) 1752 202301
ORDERS FAX: 44 (0) 1752 202333
ORDERS E-MAIL:
enquiries@nbninternational.com

Every effort has been made to contact copyright holders; in the event of an error or omission, please notify the publisher.

University of Toronto Press acknowledges the financial assistance to its publishing program of the Canada Council for the Arts and the Ontario Arts Council, an agency of the Government of Ontario.

Printed in the United States of America.

CONTENTS

List of Illustrations vii

Note on Transliteration ix

Acknowledgements xi

Map xii

1   Introduction 1

2   Tournaments of Change: Socialism, Awakening,
    Transition, Post-socialism 7

3   Loss, Memory, and Religion 21

4   Identity, Nationalism, and Community-making 35

5   Political Culture, Democracy, and Protest 47

6   Gender, Sex, and Desire 61

7   Media and Art 73

8   Russia Beyond Russia 87

Glossary 101

References 105

Index 113

ILLUSTRATIONS

2.1. Russian traders buying gold in the "open market"..........................18
3.1. Young woman wearing a Soviet military cap in 2011.....................26
3.2. Russians posing with Lenin and Stalin in 2008.
The boy wears a Young Pioneers scarf..27
5.1. Moscow, 2013. Preparing for a demonstration 57
7.1. Cover page of one of *chto delat*'s newspapers 79

NOTE ON TRANSLITERATION

In this book I employ the Library of Congress system of transliteration, except when another spelling has become commonly accepted in English (e.g., *glasnost* instead of *glasnost'*, or *Chernobyl* instead of *Chornobyl'*, or *Novaya Gazeta* instead of *Novaia Gazeta*).

ACKNOWLEDGEMENTS

This book started its life as a series of lectures I prepared for an undergradu-
ate course entitled "The Anthropology of Socialism." I would like to thank
the students who participated in this course, as well as Varun Puri and
Valentina Tomov for encouraging me to bring this book to life. I would
also like to thank two anonymous reviewers for their helpful comments,
and for reaffirming that this has been a project worth doing. I wrote this
book in the last two years as chair of the Department of Anthropology,
a time marked by a number of taxing events. I would like to thank Karin
Bauer, Amber Dean, Cole Gately, Grace Kehler, Susie O'Brien, Tony Porter,
and Vilma Rossi for their friendship and support, and Bart de Cort for
holding steady the line between work and everything else.

Contemporary Russia

CHAPTER 1

INTRODUCTION

Why an introduction to the anthropology of Russia? There certainly exist a number of very good introductions to Russian history, politics, governance, economics, thought, and art. However, as interesting and insightful as many of these are, none of them has been designed to assist readers in exploring the anthropology of Russia. The goal of this book is to provide students with an introduction to the study of the anthropology of Russia, especially as it has emerged in approximately the last 20 years. Working from concrete **ethnographic** studies, theoretically informed descriptions of particular ways of life, I hope to familiarize readers with some of the themes of this field, and to provide them with a working knowledge of the conceptual and analytical tools used by anthropologists to understand these topics.

Methodologically, anthropologists tend to draw on **fieldwork**—a form of long-term residence in particular communities—and on **participant observation**—a form of immersion in the world of others—as their core research practices. In arguing that this methodology assists them in understanding people's actions from their own point of view, anthropologists also speak of an **emic** approach to **culture**. One reason that anthropology is so exciting is that it asks us to move beyond common sense assumptions about cultures, peoples, and places in order to critically reflect on our own cultural and social routines.

Although fieldwork remains anthropology's key approach, anthropologists of Russia have nevertheless greatly expanded their methodological arsenal by conducting research in historical archives, recognizing the analytical importance of photography and other forms of visual culture

(Shevchenko 2014), and acknowledging the importance of online media sources (Gray 2016). They have also ventured into the arena of literature to understand how fiction may help them to dive deeper into particular cultural imaginations. For example, in her book on Russian cottage life (*dachnaia zhizn'*) Melissa Caldwell (2010) cites the late-nineteenth-century Russian writer Anton Chekhov as a key informant, and Kirin Narayan (2012) has even taken up Chekhov as her ethnographic muse. Aleksandr Pushkin's poem "Prisoner of the Caucasus" assumes a central position in Bruce Grant's (2009) exploration of those cultural understandings that frame Russia's Caucasus region as always already "forbidden" and "dark." And Michele Rivkin-Fish and Elena Trubina's (2010) collaboration on analyses of nationality and cultural diversity in Russia serves as a good example of the ways in which cultural analysts have started to work in interdisciplinary and allied ways (see also Baiburin, Kelly, and Vakhtin 2012).

Approaching the Anthropology of Russia

Geographically, the contemporary Russian Federation is the largest country in the world. Covering a territory of approximately 17 million square kilometers, and occupying nearly a third of the Eurasian landmass, it stretches over 11 time zones: from the Bering Strait in the east to the Baltic Sea in the west, and from the polar regions of the Russian North to the semi-deserts of the Caspian Sea in the south. As a multinational federation, Russia accommodates a population of 142.4 million, comprising more than 180 peoples, 40 of whom are legally recognized as indigenous. To put this into anthropological terms: Russia does not constitute a culturally homogenous entity but disaggregates into various "Russias"—into a multiplicity of cultural, political, religious, and economic ways of being. It is for this reason that in this book Russia does not mark an uncomplicated object of analysis that can be studied from a single and stable location, but a richly diverse place that can be approached from a number of perspectives.

Given the welter of English-language anthropological articles and books that in the mid-1990s began to emerge on the anthropology of Russia, it is easy to think that as a distinct field of inquiry the anthropology of Russia marks a rather recent phenomenon. Yet as both Russian and non-Russian anthropologists (Balzer 1995; Gray, Vakhtin, and Schweitzer 2003; Anderson and Arzyutov 2016) have pointed out, the anthropology of Russia is neither a recent nor a Western phenomenon, although—as Sergey Sokolovskiy (2011) has suggested—the paucity of institutional support for anthropologists in Russia is increasingly putting the discipline in danger. In particular the fact that funding for research in Russia has been mainly forthcoming from institutions located in Western Europe and North America has produced a certain lopsidedness in research production. This reality has ushered in a number of criticisms by non-Western colleagues who argue that their research insights are not always acknowledged (Cervinkova 2012). More than an internal quarrel in the anthropology of Russia, such criticisms are also linked to broader discussions in anthropology: What are the constellations of cultural and political power that produce and reproduce research inequalities? How can and do anthropologists challenge such inequalities? Even though I do not tackle these questions directly in this book, I have sought to stay mindful of their implications throughout the writing process.

Approaching Culture in the Anthropology of Russia

As I briefly mentioned above, the concept of culture is at the heart of anthropology—and it is notoriously hard to define. Most anthropologists, though, tend to agree that culture constitutes a complex and interconnected whole that includes history, economics, sexuality and gender, morality and religion, identity, tradition, and art. While at first glance such a definition may appear to be frustratingly broad, to anthropologists it offers the advantage of recognizing that culture is not a natural given but constructed and "made-up." This is not to say that people do not experience culture as meaningful and real, but rather to signal the fact that historical, material, political, and social conditions all help to shape and construct culture. It is also for this reason that anthropologists argue that culture cannot be reduced to a few **essentialist** features, but is always open and contingent.

Cultural analysts have argued and shown that culture comes in many forms. For example, culture exists in the form of capital-C or *high culture*—that is, in the form of culture associated with Russian operas, the Bolshoi ballet, and the novels of Fyodor Dostoyevsky; *folk culture*—which refers to those cultural products and practices that have developed over time within a particular community or socially identifiable group and that are communicated from generation to generation and among people who tend to be known to one another; *mass culture*—a form of culture that tends to be produced for an unknown and disparate audience, and frequently relies on electronic or mechanical media to reach the largest possible audience; and *everyday culture (byt')*, with "everyday" comprising all those cultural activities concerned with the production of daily meaning: shopping, remembering, working, talking, watching TV, and surfing on the internet. In their ethnographic analyses anthropologists of Russia have relied on all of these categories and have creatively drawn on them in intermeshed ways.

As historians of Russia (Kelly, Pilkington, Shepherd, and Volkov 1998) remind us, it is difficult to identify the precise moment when the study of culture became an important intellectual project in the study of Russia.

The 1724 formation of the Academy of Sciences by Tsar Peter the Great (1672–1725)—an intrepid traveler who sought to connect Russia more closely with European **Enlightenment** ideals—as well as the 1845 inauguration of the Russian Geographical Society, were major steps in establishing the study of culture as a distinct academic field. Paired with Russia's desires for colonial expansion and empire-making, the geographers and botanists (Krasheninnikov, Müller, Gmelin) of the Great Northern or Second Kamchatka Expedition (1733–43; the first Kamchatka Expedition took place from 1725–30) not only began to map the Arctic Coast of Siberia and some parts of the North American coastline, but also opened up the desire for more expeditions and expansion. Ethnographic museums began to emerge in Russian centers, displaying the peoples and cultures of the Russian empire. Ethnographic journals began to offer scientific insights and descriptions. In the 1870s Russian ethnographer Nikolai Miklukho-Maklai, after whom the Institute of Anthropology and Ethnography of the Moscow branch of the Russian Academy of Sciences is named, began to conduct ethnographic work beyond the borders of Imperial Russia, most notably in New Guinea, Melanesia, and Polynesia.

Toward the end of the nineteenth century members of the Russian **intelligentsia**—meaning those who were educated but also saw themselves in critical opposition to an authoritarian regime—began to conduct "cultural work" (*kul'turnaia rabota*) among workers and peasants by teaching them in self-organized workshops and schools. As one consequence, understandings of culture began to move beyond their heretofore predominantly agricultural connotations to signify values that could be acquired, transmitted, and taught. In the 1880s culture came to be associated with "enlightenment" (*prosveshchenie*), "education," "civilization," and "spirituality" (*dukhovnost'*), as well as with "being well-educated" (*obrazovannyi*) and "well-bred" (*vospitannyi*). As Bruce Grant (1995) has shown, these meanings were also used to distinguish supposedly more "cultured" Russians from the supposedly unsophisticated cultures of Russia's indigenous peoples and peasants. As these constituencies were considered "less mannered," "backward," and "primitive," their level of "culturedness" (*kul'turnost'*, loosely translated as "cultured behavior") became the site of much political attention and significance. For example, in 1930 in Leningrad (now St. Petersburg) the Institute of the Peoples of the North under the leadership of Russian ethnographer Vladimir Bogoraz began to train indigenous teachers for Russia's utmost northern regions.

It seems clear that from its very beginning the **Soviet Union** (for a discussion see Chapter 1) recognized the importance of culture in facilitating the construction of a new historical era and country. Innovative developments in academic research and literature, film, theater, and sculpture abounded in early Soviet Russia. With the emergence of **Stalinism** (see Chapter 3) by the end of the 1920s, culture came to be more linked to material rewards, including pay, holidays, and apartments. In the post-World War II era, it slowly became associated with the "Soviet way of life" (*sovetskii obraz zhizni*) as the supposed source of the superiority of the socialist system, evinced—for example—by the Soviet Union's 1957 launching of Sputnik as the world's first artificial satellite. Away from the culture of heroism that had marked the beginning of the Soviet Union, the "Soviet way of life" also indexed an increase in the importance of the private sphere: a move toward domestic life. In the mid-1980s years of **perestroika** (restructuring) and **glasnost** (transparency; for a discussion of both terms see Chapter 1) the role of culture changed again. Now its primary function was no longer to provide serenity, leisure, or amusement, but to facilitate reflection and debate. In the name of *glasnost*, libraries opened closed stacks, museums began to show images that heretofore would have been considered risqué, and for the first time governmental policies and decisions were publicly discussed.

How to Use This Book

I should probably tell you a few things about how this book was written, and about how to use it. In the beginning, I have to admit, I felt somewhat hesitant to embark on this project. In my own teaching I tend to shy away from using introductory texts, preferring book-length ethnographies as the central texts of a given course. One reason for this approach is that I wish for students who participate in my classes to gain a feel for the extraordinary analytical labor that goes into the crafting of ethnography. At the same time, however, I also recognize that a great number of students tend to long for introductory texts that may serve as a base from which to further explore issues and themes pertinent to—for example—the anthropology of Russia. As a researcher and teacher, I am inspired by the investigative richness the anthropology of Russia has to offer. A book like this cannot be definitive, but I do hope that it provides you with tools, concepts, ideas, and examples that will allow you to independently embark on further investigations.

In this book I have incorporated a number of pedagogical features. In consultation with students and instructors, and based on my own sense of teaching, *Russia: Anthropological Insights* condenses a welter of material into seven themes, each of which corresponds to a current area of interest in the anthropology of Russia. Each chapter works from concrete anthropological research and includes at least one *ethnographic close-up* to provide an in-depth exploration of a key concept or theme. While I've listed anthropological literature directly referenced in a given chapter in the final section of this book, I've listed original works by anthropologists and other scholars who deal with the same material in a different way or with a different emphasis at the end of each respective chapter. Each chapter is followed by a number of short discussion questions. Important terms are highlighted in **bold** on their first appearance in the text and recorded in a glossary at the end of the book to allow readers to cross-reference with ease.

Suggested Discussion Questions

What is your view on culture? How would you define it—or, what kind of definition do you prefer and why? How is the term "culture" used to distinguish groups of people from each other? How would you describe your own experience of being part of culture?

Suggestions for Further Reading

Appadurai, Arjun. 2000. "Grassroots Globalization and the Research Imagination." *Public Culture* 12 (1): 1–19. https://doi.org/10.1215/08992363-12-1-1.

Balzer, Marjorie M., ed. 1992. *Russian Traditional Culture: Religion, Gender, and Customary Law*. New York: M. E. Sharpe.

Barker, Adele, and Bruce Grant, eds. 2010. *The Russia Reader: History, Culture, Politics*. Durham: Duke University Press.

Bressler, Michael L., ed. 2009. *Understanding Contemporary Russia*. Boulder: Lynne Rienner.

Gupta, Akhil, and James Ferguson. 1997. "Discipline and Practice: 'The Field' as Site, Method, and Location in Anthropology." In *Anthropological Locations: Boundaries and Grounds of a Field Science*, edited by Akhil Gupta and James Ferguson, 1–46. Berkeley: University of California Press.

Kelly, Catriona. 1998. *Russian Cultural Studies: An Introduction*. Oxford: Oxford University Press.

Marks, Steven G. 2013. *How Russia Shaped the Modern World: From Art to Anti-Semitism, Ballet, to Bolshevism*. Princeton: Princeton University Press.

Ostrovsky, Arkady. 2015. *The Invention of Russia*. New York: Viking.

Rzhevsky, Nicholas, ed. 2012. *The Cambridge Companion to Modern Russian Culture*. Cambridge: Cambridge University Press. https://doi.org/10.1017/CCOL9781107002524.

TOURNAMENTS OF CHANGE: SOCIALISM, AWAKENING, TRANSITION, POST-SOCIALISM

Ethnographic Close-Up

In early January 1992, I was standing on the square in front of Moscow's *Manezh*, a large oblong building in the immediate neighborhood of the Kremlin and the Red Square. Today Manezh Square is an enormous and luxurious shopping mall, but in the beginning of the 1990s it was a large open space with congested traffic around its edges and cars randomly parked throughout the middle of the square. It also doubled as an unlawful space for exchanging foreign currencies, especially US dollars, into rubles. At that time I was poised to visit the northern Kamchatka peninsula in the Russian Far East, and friends in Moscow had warned me that *there* I would certainly not be able exchange money. (Of course, once I arrived in Kamchatka it turned out that the peninsula enjoyed its own illegal and underground spheres.) After having mentally sorted through a number of people—mostly men—all wrapped in coats of dark shades, I approached one of them standing at the edge of the square. He was holding a package of *papirosy* (cigarettes without filters) with a small $ sign sticking out of it in his hands, identifying him as one of the marketeers. There was a bit of back and forth between us as we negotiated the exchange rate, and then there was a bit of back and forth when he ordered another man to get the money. That day I returned with several plastic bags full of cash to my room at the *Gostinitsa Akademii Nauk* (Hotel of the Academy of Sciences), where many foreign academics stayed at the end of the 1980s and beginning of the 1990s.

I take this vignette as my jumping-off point to discuss both the speed and intensity of the political, economic, and cultural changes that took place in Russia between 1985 and roughly 2000. In calling this chapter "Tournaments of Change," I build on anthropologist Arjun Appadurai's (1986) insight that cultural and historical change does not serenely and steadily move along a linear line, but is marked by uneven temporal dynamics. In trying to capture a sense of the distinctiveness of the temporalities of change, I've organized this chapter around four registers: "socialism," "awakening," "transition," and "post-socialism." A brief historical overview precedes the discussion of each register to better situate its ethnographic and experiential components in their appropriate temporal and social contexts. These registers do not always and necessarily constitute distinct categories but overlap as events unfold.

Socialism

An Extremely Brief History of the Soviet Union

Following on the heels of the economic costs of World War I (1914–18) and the February 1917 food riots in Petrograd, in March 1917 Tsar Nicholas II abdicates the throne. A provisional government is created. On October 24–25, 1917, Bolshevik and Left Socialist revolutionaries stage a coup, occupying government buildings and other strategic points. A new government composed mainly of Bolshevik commissars is formed. The aims of the Bolshevik Revolution—liquidating the capitalist economic system, increasing public wealth, and raising the material and cultural standards of working-class people—enjoy wide appeal among workers and among parts of the peasantry. However, a strong opposition exists as well, and from 1918–21 the Red (Bolshevik) Army is engulfed in a brutal civil war against the White Army (monarchists, liberals, moderate socialists, peasants seeking freedom from the state, and non-Russians). After the three ruinous years of "war communism," in 1922 the first Soviet Russian government introduces the "new economic policy," which represents a short-lived phase of market-oriented economic policies, allowing private individuals to own small enterprises, while the Soviet State continues to control banks, foreign trade, and large industries. In the same year the new Union of Soviet Socialist Republics is formally established, and in 1923 the Soviet Union raises its most official symbol— a red flag featuring a gold-bordered star and a crossed gold hammer and sickle in the upper left corner—for the first time. In January 1924 Lenin, one of the revolution's foremost theorists and head of the first Soviet Russian government, dies. A protracted power struggle for the Soviet leadership ensues. Joseph Stalin, a Georgian-born revolutionary and strong supporter of the formation of the Cheka, a secret police organization that becomes the forerunner of the Soviet Union and Russia's secret police, rises to power.

In seeking a revolution from above, Stalin seeks to modernize the economy. In the name of industrialization, production plants for aluminum and nonferrous metals are constructed, and hydroelectric and fuel-operated power stations are built across the country. In 1928 Stalin puts the Soviet Union's first five-year plan—a managerial tool that emphasizes the importance of central planning for economic growth—in motion. Expanding the plan in 1929, Stalin is also responsible for the creation of the collective farm (*kolkhoz*) system, which becomes the Soviet Union's key agricultural unit. The forced implementation of the *kolkhoz* system is accompanied by a campaign to liquidate the *kulaks*—supposedly wealthy peasants—and by the confiscation of peasants' property, including animals and land. As resistance mounts, millions of people are arrested and exiled to Siberia, Central Asia, or the Far North. In 1937–38, the Moscow "show trials" take place, in which score of defendants are accused of crimes against Stalin or the Soviet state, and sentenced to death.

9

When in September 1953 Nikita Khrushchev (1894–1971) becomes the First Secretary of the Communist Party of the Soviet Union, a number of Stalin's policies are reversed. In general Khrushchev pursues a politics of "peaceful coexistence" with the **West**, and his initial policy of de-Stalinization has widespread repercussions in the country. In 1956, Khrushchev delivers his famous "Secret Speech," in which he denounces the violent excesses of the Stalin era. But 1956 is also the year in which the Soviet army violently puts down an uprising in Hungary; crackdowns on **dissidents**—women and men who openly oppose Soviet official policies—begin to intensify. In 1964 Khrushchev is removed from power and replaced by Party Secretary Leonid Brezhnev (1906–82). In 1968 the Soviet army invades Czechoslovakia to obstruct a series of liberalizing reforms collectively known as the Prague Spring. In 1975 the Soviet Union becomes one of the signatories of the Helsinki Accords, a series of diplomatic guidelines and rules to improve relations between the Communist Bloc and the West. Nevertheless, in a highly controversial move, in 1979 Soviet troops invade Afghanistan to support the country's non-Islamist military government. Three years later, in November 1982, Brezhnev dies of a heart attack. Yuri Andropov, the former head of the Committee for State Security (KGB), succeeds him. In 1984 Andropov dies of renal failure, and in 1985, Konstantin Chernenko, who had replaced him, dies of emphysema.

Although the anthropology of Russia recognizes the deep complexities of the history of the Soviet Union, there nevertheless exist two key tendencies in examining **socialism**'s cultural, economic, and political articulations. A complex political idea based on the late-nineteenth-century writings of Karl Marx and Friedrich Engels, broadly speaking socialism indexes a propensity for public rather than private ownership of material resources. In particular if adopted by a **state** (see Chapter 5), socialism also indexes a system of *instrumental rationality*: a system based on a belief in economic and technological progress and cultural forms of standardization. Given the significance socialism placed on the economic sphere, one approach is thus to understand the ways in which socialist principles underwrote and shaped the Soviet economy, including the effects of collectivizing people's **means of production** (tools, factories, technological facilities, machinery, equipment, and animals and land). Another approach is to center on **ideology** to understand how Soviet cultural practices supported the ideas and ideals of the Soviet Union.

In its most classic form the first approach is exemplified by Caroline Humphrey's (1983) study of two collective farms—both of which were named in honor of Karl Marx—in the 1960s in Buryatia. Humphrey shows that the Communist Party did not completely control these collective farms' production processes, although it often claimed to do so. For example, in Buryatia farm officials were able to suffuse supposedly rational production processes with kinship-based and spiritual practices, and they also creatively changed and negotiated unrealistic plan targets. In a similar vein, Nikolai Ssorin-Chaikov (2003) describes how indigenous Evenki reindeer herders in northern Siberia managed to evade the managerial practices of the bureaucratic state by maintaining their own cultural practices. In this way, both Humphrey and Ssorin-Chaikov demonstrate that Soviet state socialism did not always already index a **totalitarian** form of government, but that it marked a more open and porous system than many negative assessments would have us believe.

At the most general level, ideology refers to those processes that directly or indirectly mask or hide the forces that make political life seem unchangeable, or—as anthropologists say—by which values and beliefs become "naturalized." Alexei Yurchak (2006) exemplifies the second approach by examining how in the period of late socialism (mid-1950s–1980s), socialist ideology became "hypernormalized"—that is, so normalized that neither political commentators nor ordinary Russians believed in the end of the Soviet Union. For example, in looking at how in special training sessions party cadres acquired the skill to produce political speeches and texts through the endless repetition of uplifting but ultimately meaningless phrases, Yurchak points to the ways in which the Soviet Union retained people's beliefs in its stability through particular forms of ritualized speechwriting. In highlighting the performative dimensions of language, he also reveals how the supposed endurance of the Soviet Union rested on political scripts that simply claimed the durability of the Soviet Union, without any real meaning being attached to them.

While from an analytically rather conventional perspective socialism and capitalism tend to represent two politically and economically antagonistic systems—socialism is totalitarian and capitalism is democratic; socialism is marked by oppression and capitalism by freedom; socialism is immoral and capitalism denoted by the recognition of human rights—Stephen Collier (2011) argues that the two systems share more forms and structures in common than we tend to assume. For example, in centering on the ways in which the assembly-line efficiency of Taylorized modes of production existed in both the United States and the Soviet Union, Collier shows that both socialist and capitalist economic systems were built on similar bureaucratic forms of rationalism. In a similar argument historian Kate Brown (2015) focuses on the ways in which in both the Soviet Union and the United States city spaces were constructed in angular ways. In comparing city plans in Karaganda, Kazakhstan, with city plans in Billings, Montana, Brown demonstrates that the infrastructural patterning of both places relies on parallel administrative modes. Of course, from an anthropological perspective these insights do not mean that we should neglect to pay attention to the particularities of the Soviet system, but neither does it mean that socialist and capitalist cultural and economic logics always already differ.

Awakening: *Perestroika* and *Glasnost*

A Brief History of Perestroika *and* Glasnost

In 1985 Mikhail Gorbachev assumes the position of General Secretary of the Communist Party. In this position he initiates two major reforms, respectively called *perestroika* (restructuring) and *glasnost* (openness). In the economic sphere, these reforms include the restitution of land to farmers and peasants after 60 years of collectivized agriculture, as well as the introduction of joint ventures with Western business partners. One of Gorbachev's first moves toward recognizing a role for non-state economic enterprises in the Soviet Union is the 1986 Law on Individual Economic Activity that legalizes individual and family-based economic efforts, including the driving of taxis, repairing of cars, and private tutoring of students. In the arena of *glasnost*, reforms include the creation of a new legislative assembly (the Congress of People's Deputies), the liberation of prisoners, and the progressive restoration of political pluralism and freedom of speech. The distribution of Georgian director Tengiz Abuladze's 1986 film *Pokaianie* (Repentance), which addresses the brutality of Stalinist terror, and the 1989 publication of Aleksandr Solzhenitsyn's heretofore censored novel *The Gulag Archipelago*, mark two major events. Gorbachev also decides to withdraw Soviet troops from Afghanistan.

One of the major historical changes initiated by *perestroika* and *glasnost* is the end of the **Cold War** (1945–89). The Cold War is the name for a number of geopolitical tensions that after World War II (1939–45) make up the international order, most notably between the "Eastern Bloc" (the Soviet Union and its satellite states) and the "Western Bloc" (the United States and its NATO [North Atlantic Treaty Organization] allies). These tensions are usually described as "cold" because for the duration of the Cold War no large-scale fighting took place between the two blocs, although both sides supported regional wars known as "proxy wars." In the Soviet context, the end of the Cold War precipitates the dissolution of the Soviet Union and state socialist regimes in Eastern Europe, but this "ending" is not without its own conflicts and tensions. In 1988 in the Caucasus, Armenians in the mountainous Karabakh region, which is part of the Soviet republic of Azerbaijan, take to the streets to demand a merger with the Soviet republic of Armenia. A significant number of Azerbaijanis understand the desires of Azerbaijan's Armenian minority as an assault on the republic's territorial integrity. As tensions escalate, pogroms targeting the Armenian population in the Azerbaijan cities of Sumgait and Baku take place. In 1990, the Baltic republics of Lithuania, Estonia, and Latvia, followed by Armenia, Azerbaijan, and Georgia, irrevocably break away from the Soviet Union.

In yielding to the Soviet republics' demands for greater autonomy, in the summer of 1991 Gorbachev agrees to a new union treaty. Before it can be signed, on August 19, a group of high-ranking Communist Party officials attempt to seize power in a coup known as "the putsch." Calling themselves the General Committee on the State of Emergency, they suspend all political activity, ban most newspapers, and put Gorbachev—who at that time is vacationing in the Crimea—under house arrest. In Moscow, thousands of protestors take to the street to actively protest the putsch in front of the Russian Federation's parliamentary building. After three days, the putsch collapses, and on August 24 Gorbachev dissolves the Central Committee of the Communist Party and resigns as its leader.

In a number of dramatic and parallel developments, in 1990 Boris Yeltsin (1931–2007), former First Secretary of the Moscow City Committee and an elected member of the Congress of People's Deputies, emerges in the spotlight of the political area. In the wake of Gorbachev's dwindling influence, in June 1991 Yeltsin is elected as the president of the Russian Federation. On December 8, the leaders of Russia, Ukraine, and Belarus sign the Belazheva Accords, effectively declaring the dissolution of the Soviet Union and the establishment of the Commonwealth of Independent States (CIS). In late December 1991 Gorbachev tenders his resignation as leader of the Soviet Union, and on the night of December 25 the Kremlin's Soviet flag is lowered for the last time. The Russian tricolor is raised in its place.

While *glasnost* exposed many unknown facts about the Soviet past, it also meant that Soviet Russia was waking up to many of its social problems, including economic mismanagement, the war in Afghanistan, and environmental disaster. As Adriana Petryna (2002) shows, one key event in the Soviet Union's discovery of what was wrong with its system was the Chernobyl disaster. On April 26, 1986, Unit Four of the Chernobyl nuclear power reactor exploded in Ukraine, spewing radioactive dust into the atmosphere that quickly grew into a cloud, spreading over Belarus, Ukraine, Russia, Scandinavia, and other parts of Western Europe. The incident itself was first noticed on April 28 in Sweden, where high levels of radioactivity were measured and traced back to Chernobyl. In the Soviet media, officials were laboring under the protection of a news blackout to downplay and curtail the effects of the disaster, and eighteen days elapsed before Mikhail Gorbachev appeared on television to fully acknowledge the catastrophe. In the meantime tens of thousands were exposed to radioactive iodine-131, which is rapidly absorbed in the thyroid. As Petryna records, **13** one consequence was the massive onset of thyroid cancer even years after the event. Soviet administrators also downplayed the extent of radioactive distribution and its clouds, describing Chernobyl as a "controlled biomedical crisis." Furthermore, accounts of injuries were limited to biomedical measures derived from a group of acute accident victims in the first few weeks following the disaster, limiting Soviet government liability for large parts of the population that were not screened or that were made vulnerable by radiation-related injuries. As the disaster of Chernobyl underscored the Soviet state's governmental irresponsibility in relation to its own population, it also underscored the state of collapse that in 1991 would bring down the Soviet Union.

Based on cultural and semiotic analyses of Russian speech in the last years of *perestroika*, Nancy Ries (1997) shows that Russians articulated and negotiated the extraordinary historical changes that began to take place in the mid-1980s through the continual exchange of stories. These stories are focused and intense, and they reflect the varied and at times paradoxical sense of powerlessness, outrage, absurdity, cynicism, and fear that people experienced then. For example, in describing how Russians talked about their almost heroic feats of procuring butter, toilet paper, and clothes in a world of seemingly never-ending shortages, Ries reveals the tensions that existed between the grandiosity of state rhetoric and everyday economic life. As she describes it, Russian narratives about daily suffering assumed an almost ritualistic dimension, in the sense that their repetitive character provided a certain commonality and release from the burdens of daily life.

Transition

A Very Brief History of the Transition

On January 2, 1992, the Russian government abandons price subsidies for most Soviet goods, effectively allowing market forces to determine prices. Price liberalization leads to massive and destabilizing inflation: people's savings disappear overnight, and significant segments of Russia's population are propelled into poverty. In finding itself at the mercy of international lenders, including the International Monetary Fund (IMF) and World Bank, the Russian government initiates a series of economic reforms—stabilization (hard budget constraints and a convertible currency), liberalization (domestic market competition and export-oriented production), and privatization (denationalization and deregulation)—collectively known as "shock therapy." As state revenues fall, public services, from the distribution of state pensions to trash collections, decline. People's salaries are not paid for months. *Blat'*—an informal economic exchange and barter system (Ledeneva 1998)—turns into an integral part of everyday life.

14   Fueled by internal differences over the proper course of Russian economic policies, political ambitions, and personal antagonisms, in the early fall of 1993 Russia enters a constitutional crisis. On September 21, President Yeltsin dissolves the Russian parliament, although he is not empowered to do so. His opponents, including former vice president Aleksandr Rutskoi, call Yeltsin's actions a *coup d'état* and vote to depose him. Rutskoi is sworn in as Russia's acting president, and Yeltsin's opponents occupy Russia's parliament building. The situation escalates. On October 3 armed supporters of the parliament try to storm the headquarters of the Russian TV center in Ostankino in Moscow. On October 4 army troops follow Yeltsin's orders and begin to shell Russia's parliament building, which at that time is occupied by a significant number of Rutskoi's supporters, from tanks. In the late afternoon of that very day, the building is in flames and Yeltsin's opponents surrender. The conflict lasts for another 10 days; approximately 160 people are killed, and several hundred are wounded.

In 1996 presidential elections are held in Russia. Yeltsin's political and economic record is under withering critique, but with significant help from the media and the **oligarchs**—extremely wealthy businessmen who have gained much of their affluence and power in the wake of the dissolution of the Soviet Union—Yeltsin is elected again. In 1998 the Russian government defaults on its international debts, and the ruble is devalued again. In May 1999 parliamentary opposition forces charge Yeltsin with unconstitutional activities, including the signing of the Belavezha Accords, the 1993 coup, and initiation of the first war in Chechnya (see Chapter 4). Yeltsin survives his opponents' attempt to impeach him. On December 31, 1999, by way of a televised seasonal greeting to the nation, Yeltsin steps down as president and passes on the reins of power to Vladimir Putin.

Following on the heels of the tumultuous changes that happened in the wake of *perestroika,* throughout the 1990s Russia faced two challenges: first, the creation of a new political structure to replace the single-party system of the Soviet Union, and second, the building of a new economic system to replace the communist command economy. It is for these reasons that economists and policy makers have dubbed the "bold 1990s" the period of "the **transition**." Anthropologists are deeply critical of the term (Wedel 1998; Hemment 2007). While acknowledging that in the 1990s Russia was a resource-scarce environment in which nascent democratic and **civil society** (see Chapter 5) organizations greatly depended on foreign funding (as they do today), they also recognize that during "the transition" foreign donor organizations began to shape Russian democracy in the image of Western-style economic and political structures.

While Western policy makers tended and tend to speak of 1990s Russia in terms of transition, Russian citizens themselves preferred to resort to the term *bespredel*, a word that indicates the absence of any shared rules or laws. As Margaret Paxson (2005) points out, Russians also frequently turned to terms such as *razrukha* (destruction), *razrushenie* (havoc), and *razlozhenie* (decomposition) to describe their experience of the economic and political disorder that had begun to mark their lives. In Russian the prefix *raz* signifies a destabilizing force, an experience of "coming loose or unstuck." It was also in the 1990s that *chernukha* (literally: that which is made dark), a slang term that had emerged in the 1980s to articulate a certain tendency toward negativity and pessimism in *glasnost* mass media and arts, came to be associated with *krizis* (crisis) as an everyday and routine occurrence (Shevchenko 2009).

As Russia was literally and symbolically falling apart, Russians' desire for stability and security grew. For example, Olga Shevchenko (2009) describes how for fear of break-ins in Moscow people began to replace their old wooden doors with steel doors, or—if that was not possible—to fortify them with at least two locks. Relatively cheap, *rakushki* (shells), car shelters assembled out of several sheets of steel that could hold everything from cars to window frames, began to line the walls of courtyards. As a material and outward sign of people's need for stability and protection, *rakushki* also doubled as signs of people's increasing emotional distance from the state. As the Russian populace grew increasingly aware that they were no longer able to rely on the state for particular services and provisions (see also Chapter 3), each individual's economic ability to take care of him or herself as well as a family became equated with autonomy and economic emancipation.

Transition, Globalization, and Consumption

As cultural analysts (Barker 1999; Beumers 2005) have pointed out, in the era of "the transition" **globalization** also reached Russia. At its most basic level, globalization is the name for the social, political, cultural, economic, and technological processes that, taken together, have created the conditions of our interconnected present. Although within the Russian context globalization tends to be considered a recent phenomenon, the movement of people and goods across national boundaries existed already in Russian imperial and Soviet times (see Chapter 8). For example, in his discussion of the 1960s and 1970s trend among Soviet music lovers to tape-record and distribute foreign jazz and rock records brought by diplomats or sailors into the country, Alexei Yurchak (2006) suggests that the Soviet Union was culturally more open and porous than conventionally envisioned. As audio-recording technologies and other techniques of media reproduction that were cheap and mobile increased, so did knowledge of music and its genres. In 1990s Russia North American serials such as *Santa Barbara*, *Dynasty*, *Dallas*, and *The X-Files*, as well as Mexican telenovelas such as *Just Maria*, *Wild Rose*, and *The Rich Also Cry*, became tremendously popular.

16   With the demise of the Soviet Union international companies and corporations were increasingly able to expand their reach into Russia and to augment the range of Russia's consumer markets. In *Consumption and Change in a Post-Soviet Middle Class* Jennifer Patico (2008) describes the ways in which teachers in St. Petersburg responded to newly emergent forms of advertising, product packaging, design, and shop window display. In a particularly telling example Patico relates how Nastia, a friend with whom she went shopping for new clothes, seriously began to dislike shopping at the *veshchovaia iarmarka*, a common kind of marketplace in Russia that sells clothes that tend to be unfashionable, of poor quality, and cheap. Deeply sensitive and responsive to the economic and cultural changes that in the 1990s started to occur in Russia—including changes in Russia's fashion industry, which began to experience the influx of foreign fashion houses such as Gucci, Louis Vuitton, Prada, and Chanel—Nastia became highly aware of the value of fashion as a **commodity** and marker of social position. Many of the garments sold at the *veshchovaia iarmarka* hailed from Turkey, a country that in Nastia's perception was "uncultured," especially if compared with the grace and style of the Italian fashions that had begun to appear in St. Petersburg's fancy boutiques. As one consequence, Nastia began to reject clothes that would not make her look culturally sophisticated and refined. In other words, in desiring and working hard to be seen as a "cultured" self, Nastia began to use clothes as an expression of cultural and social distinction.

In her analysis, Patico draws on the work of French sociologist Pierre Bourdieu (1930–2002). For Bourdieu, whenever we consume something—be it clothes, food, images, music, or art—we are engaging in complex forms of social differentiation and display, whether we realize it or not. We may be aware of this social game of distinction as, for example, Nastia was when she began to choose clothes that made her look "cultured," but for Bourdieu we even participate in the game when we make decisions that seem to express individual or personal choices. To understand such processes of **conspicuous consumption**—consumption that is obvious, noticeable, and visible in order to signal or symbolize class differences and distinctions—anthropologists also draw on the notion of commodity fetishism:

the literal attribution of a magical or sexual power to a commodity. In essence, commodities are objects and services produced for exchange or consumption by someone other than their producers. As in an increasingly market-oriented and capitalist Russia material objects were more and more branded, commodities turned into symbols of meaning and value. From such a perspective, in Russia (as elsewhere), commodities began to signify relationships between people while, in turn, people and social relationships become objectified. As Patico points out, for many Russians this marked a qualitatively new experience: an experience away from the non-monetary exchange systems (*blat'*) that in the 1990s were very active in Russia.   **17**

Post-socialism

A Very Brief History of Post-socialism
In the beginning of the 2000s, Vladimir Putin initially assumed the position of acting president and went on to win the March 26, 2000, presidential election. In the aftermath of the "wild 1990s," many Russians began to associate Putin's presidency with a relative sense of economic stability and safety, and he became quite popular as a result. Oil prices soared, and Russia's wage crisis—as indicated by the fact that in the 1990s wages had significantly declined, or were frequently paid in kind or not at all—disappeared. In 2004, Putin easily won re-election and, until 2008, completed a second term as Russia's president. Toward the end of his second term, Putin introduced a number of constitutional changes, which allowed him to serve as Russia's premier from 2008 to 2012, while Dmitry Medvedev assumed the position of Russia's president. In 2012, Putin was elected as president again, and in spring 2018 he won his fourth term as president, which—in all likelihood—he will complete in 2024. Critics fault the deeply controversial Putin with reintroducing a centralized political system under the mantle of democracy, including curtailing the power of domestic politicians, businesspeople and entrepreneurs, and the press.

To capture the ways in which the legacies of the Soviet Union continue to shape contemporary culture in Russia, anthropologists have tended to turn to the term **post-socialism**. Like socialism, post-socialism is a multifaceted term that encompasses a number of phenomena: political struggles over power and wealth, public anxieties about public and reproductive health (Rivkin-Fish 2005), and governmental contempt for democracy and civil society. Socially and politically post-socialism has also been equated with the term **neoliberalism**, which refers to free market economic policies, the privatization of public services, and the dismantling of the welfare state. However, given the diverse political and social trajectories of present-day life in Russia, anthropologists have

Figure 2.1 Russian traders buying gold in the "open market."
Photo by the author

started to ask if the use of the term post-socialism still makes sense. As Caroline Humphrey (2002) notes, the use of the term is appropriate as long as the citizens of Russia (and Eastern Europe) identify with or relate to the Soviet past, or recognize socialist ideas and practices as relevant for their sense of being. That is, the prefix "post" should not be taken in a literal way; the term post-socialism does not simply indicate that the time of Soviet state socialism is over, but that its legacies still haunt Russian political, cultural, and social life today.

One of the most visible and significant markers of post-socialism in Russia is the considerable disparity in the citizenry's wealth. Anthropologists have examined the emergence of this disparity as related to mafia-like corruption (Ries 2002), described in terms of *bratva* (brotherhood) and *krysha* (roof; racket); new economic identities such as the *biznesmen* (Yurchak 2003); and, in general, the "new Russians" who tend to enjoy ostentatiously flaunting their wealth rather than hiding it from public view (Humphrey 2002). Michele Rivkin-Fish (2005) has demonstrated how increasing social and economic inequalities have led to extreme differences in reproductive and other health outcomes, including rates of tuberculosis, alcohol poisoning, malnutrition, domestic abuse, and AIDS (*SPID*). In documenting how the homeless or *bomzhi (bez opredelennogo mesta zhitel'stva*, without a specific place of residence) in post-socialist St. Petersburg experience the very palpable and dire consequences of poverty, Tova Höjdestrand (2009) has described the *bomzhis'* social inability to secure necessities such as food, clothing, shelter, medical aid, and sanitation. As one consequence, the homeless are not only socially and spatially marginalized but resort to increasingly perilous places that potentially also endanger their lives.

Suggested Discussion Questions

How would you describe the experience of radical social and economic change that took place in Russia? How do people experience such change; how does it make them feel? Why did commodities become important? What constitutes the relationship between the demise of socialism and the emergence of the *bomzhi*?

Suggestions for Further Reading

Alexievich, Svetlana. 2016. *Secondhand Time: The Last of the Soviets*, translated by Bela Shayevich. New York: Random House.

Boym, Svetlana. 1994. *Common Places: Mythologies of Everyday Life in Russia*. Cambridge, MA: Harvard University Press.

Burawoy, Michael, and Katherine Verdery, eds. 1999. *Uncertain Transition: Ethnographies of Change in the Postsocialist World*. Lanham, MD: Rowman and Littlefield.

Caldwell, Melissa. 2004. *Not by Bread Alone: Social Support in the New Russia*. Berkeley: University of California Press.

Ghodsee, Kristin. 2011. *Lost in Transition: Ethnographies of Everyday Life after Communism*. Durham: Duke University Press. https://doi.org/10.1215/9780822394617.

Hann, Chris M., ed. 2002. *Postsocialism: Ideals, Ideologies, and Practices in Eurasia*. London: Routledge. https://doi.org/10.4324/9780203428115.

Humphrey, Caroline. 2002. *The Unmaking of Soviet Life: Everyday Economies after Socialism*. Ithaca, NY: Cornell University Press.

Kennedy, Michael. 2002. *Cultural Formations of Postcommunism: Emancipation, Transition, Nation, and War*. Minneapolis: University of Minnesota Press.

Ledeneva, Alena. 2006. *How Russia Really Works: The Informal Practices that Shaped Post-Soviet Politics and Business*. Ithaca, NY: Cornell University Press.

Markowitz, Fran. 2000. *Coming of Age in Post-Soviet Russia*. Chicago: University of Illinois Press.

Morris, Jeremy. 2016. *Everyday Post-Socialism: Working Class Communities in the Russian Margins*. London: Palgrave Macmillan. https://doi.org/10.1057/978-1-349-95089-8.

Roberts, Graham. 2016. *Consumer Culture, Branding, and Identity in the New Russia*. London: Routledge.

Stephenson, Svetlana. 2015. *Gangs of Russia: From the Streets to the Corridors of Power*. Ithaca, NY: Cornell University Press.

Verdery, Katherine. 1996. *What Was Socialism, and What Comes Next?* Princeton: Princeton University Press. https://doi.org/10.1515/9781400821990.

Walker, Charles. 2010. *Learning to Labour in Post-Soviet Russia: Vocational Youth in Transition.* New York: Routledge.

Weiner, Douglas R. 1999. *A Little Corner of Freedom: Russian Nature Protection from Stalin to Gorbachev.* Berkeley: University of California Press.

Wengle, Susanne A. 2015. *Post-Soviet Power: State-led Development and Russia's Marketization.* Cambridge: Cambridge University Press.

Zavisca, Jane. 2015. *Housing the New Russia.* Ithaca, NY: Cornell University Press.

20

CHAPTER 3

LOSS, MEMORY, AND RELIGION

While in the last chapter I chronicled and fleshed out some of the historical, social, and economic events that contributed to the making of present-day Russia, in this chapter I focus on three analytical registers—loss, memory, and religion—that exemplify Russians' search for **meaning** following the breakup of the Soviet Union. In this chapter meaning—a term that indexes the purpose or significance of social beliefs and actions—emerges most pointedly in the form of emotions such as mourning and grief, as well as in a belief in the sacred and divine.

I begin by exploring **loss** as a socially significant experience of separation and rupture. In his book *The Patriotism of Despair: Nation, War, and Loss in Russia* Serguei Oushakine (2009) identifies loss as a key trope by which to understand people's experiences and interpretations of the Soviet Union's disintegration. In looking at military, psychological, economic, and inter-personal events and communications that transpired in the city of Barnaul in the Altai region, Oushakine chronicles what happens when an entire cultural and political **cosmology**—the organizing logic of cultural and politically specific forms of meaning—falls apart. In drawing on Oushakine's description of the **life story** of Gennadi Uminskii, a Russian soldier who was seriously wounded in Russia's First Chechen War, I describe how emotionally and morally for Russians the collapse of the Soviet cosmology was the source of much pain: an unwished-for emotional divestment from the moral and political order of the Soviet Union. Methodologically, I also seek to convey a sense of how for anthropologists life stories—as a particular mode of representation—represent not merely accounts of an individual's life but also ways of understanding how broader social forces articulate themselves in the trajectory of that life.

Following on the heels of the tumultuous, rapid, and far-reaching changes of the transition, in the 1990s Russians increasingly started to evoke the Soviet past through the **collective memory** of Soviet artifacts, images, stories, and symbols. The term "collective memory" emerges from the writings of French sociologist Maurice Halbwachs (1992), who argued that memory is not static but malleable, and who called analysts' attention to the fact that acts of remembering are not purely driven by an interest in the past but speak to the social and political concerns of the present as well. In other words, it is not the past but the present that determines not only what we remember but, more importantly, *how* we remember it. In anthropology and related disciplines Halbwachs's insights have become important for scholars interested in the ways in which people understand their own historical and political landscape and time. This does not mean that in discussions of memory questions about historical accuracy are not important, but, rather, that they are not the driving force. If there is one question that underlies the three studies of memory that I introduce in this chapter's second section, it might be this: with all the possible versions of the past that circulate in society, how do particular accounts get established and disseminated as the public ones?

In 1990s Russia one of the most palpable and significant consequences of the Soviet Union's breakdown was the emergence of a varied landscape of **religion**, spirituality, and spiritual healing. Although in the Soviet era Russian Orthodox, Buddhist, Muslim, Jewish, and shamanic beliefs had always been observed, it was the regime's demise that showed that religion had been a far more resilient phenomenon than Soviet official atheism would have wanted us to believe (Luehrmann 2011). In briefly introducing three ethnographies interested in spiritual practices and in religion as the study of "the holy," "sacred," and "revered," I also hope to show how issues of change are endowed with particular moral and cultural meanings.

Loss

As I mentioned briefly in Chapter 2, in September 1991 Chechnya, one of the Russian Federation's Caucasus regions, declared independence. Citing a long history of antagonisms, including confrontations with Cossack settlers in the sixteenth century, the southward expansion of the Tsarist empire in the nineteenth century, and the increase of Russian settlements in the era of the Soviet Union, Chechen separatists under the leadership of Dzhokhar Dudaev argued that this declaration marked the inevitable outcome of their grievances with a series of a Russian regimes. Initially the Yeltsin government tolerated this declaration, but—in response to increasing pressures to fight the Chechen rebels—in December 1994 the Russian army invaded Chechnya. From December 1994 to March 1995, Grozny was under intense Russian bombardment, but in May 1995 a Chechen raid on the Russian city of Budennovsk began to reverse the direction of the war. Fighting continued until in August 1996 Chechen rebels gained and kept control of Grozny. On August 31, 1996, Russian and Chechen representatives signed the Khasav–Yurt accord, which stipulated the withdrawal of all federal forces from Chechnya and the demilitarization of Grozny.

In the lead-up to the August 1996 Battle of Grozny, Uminskii's platoon had been ordered to unblock several checkpoints in Grozny's center to rescue journalists and a Russian general who had been captured by the Chechens. **23** Chechen fighters encircled and killed the majority of soldiers in the platoon. Together with others, Uminskii managed to hide in a ruined building until Grozny's siege was effectively stopped. Having survived the First Chechen War, Uminskii spent the next years in Russian hospitals, recovering from concussions and shell shock. In 1998 he was released, diagnosed with a "physical disability of the second degree," which allowed him to apply for limited employment under medical supervision. Fearing that this would not be enough, Uminskii decided to secure a pension from the Ministry of Defence, but his efforts failed. He also learned that his contract with the ministry had been voided due to his alleged "long absence," and that—as his military division had been disbanded—he could not expect compensation.

To Uminskii, and countless other Russian soldiers who found themselves in similar positions, this decision marked loss and produced pain for particular reasons. As discourses and shared political and social forms of meaning were falling apart, so were principles and rules that until then had been understood as timeless and secure. Especially within the context of the Soviet army's 1945 victory in World War II—or the Great Patriotic War—war had assumed a ritualized sacrality that ensured that veterans were protected economically and socially, and sometimes even turned into heroes. In 2005 a regional court overturned a previous decision that had obliged the Ministry of Defence to provide financial compensation and a pension for Gennadi Uminskii, citing as its rationale that the conditions of war had made it impossible to truly determine who carried the responsibilities for Uminskii's injuries. This decision not only eroded the conditions of economic security for Gennadi Uminskii, but also exposed the fact that the old languages and moral imaginations of a Soviet cosmology were no longer in sync with those of post-Soviet Russia.

Memory

Below I introduce three examples of the ways in which Russian women and men remember the Soviet past. I look at objects, symbols, artifacts, images, monuments, celebrations, and stories in order to consider "acts of memorialization," by which I mean an active form of historical recall that, while ostensibly indexing the Soviet past, actually points to Russia's present.

Post-socialist Nostalgia

In the aftermath of the Soviet Union, to many non-Russian observers the collective sorrow and mourning that many Russians expressed at the fall of the Soviet Union and the loss of a "Soviet way of life" (*sovetskii obraz zhizni*)—including values and ideals of equality, community, selflessness, friendship, education, and work—came as a surprise. In particular Western observers often wondered why Russians tended to speak with grief and sorrow about the passing of a political system that, at least in the West, had often been spoken of as a totalitarian government. Yet in the face of an overt Western triumphalism over the demise of Soviet socialism, many Russians began to point to their positive experiences of the Soviet system: free housing, health care, and education, secure employment, and a more or less equitable distribution of monetary resources and other forms of wealth. Public transportation, clothes, books, and visits to the theater, cinema, and museum had been affordable or cheap. From the perspective of many Russians, these were aspects of a socialist reality that mattered as achievements in their own right.

Most commonly, anthropologists working in Russia have described Russians' emotional and affective attachments to the Soviet past in terms of post-socialist **nostalgia.** Coined in the late seventeenth century by the Swiss medical student Johannes Hofer, who used "nostalgia" as a compound of two Greek words—*nostos* (the return home) and *algos* (grief, pain, sorrow)—to describe the homesickness of Swiss mercenaries who fought in regions remote from their homeland, nostalgia marks a longing for something that can no longer be had: a place, a home, or a time. The cultural analyst Svetlana Boym (2001) differentiates between *restorative* and *reflective* nostalgia. While restorative nostalgia emphasizes *nostos* and, sometimes literally, seeks to rebuild lost homes, reflective nostalgia self-consciously acknowledges the distance and difference between the experiences of the past and the realities of the present. For example, in looking at artifacts ranging from Lenin badges to Soviet army regalia and cameras, Boym argues that such artifacts do not simply represent the material waste of Soviet culture, but that their post-Soviet popularity needs to be understood in terms of the emotional protection they provide: the affirmation of Soviet selves in a political context in which all things Soviet seemed to be devalued. Thus, more than indexing an uncomplicated longing for the past, post-socialist nostalgia also evinces a critical edge: people's disenchantment with their present and possibly even a longing for political alternatives that might have been and whose unrecognized potential should be recognized (Boyer 2010).

Monuments of Innocence

As Bruce Grant (2001) has shown, the Russian Federation's struggles over the meaning of the Soviet past also tend to articulate themselves in struggles over historical heritage. In examining the politics and aesthetics surrounding Moscow's 98-meter-high statue of Peter the Great, which was designed by the Georgian sculptor Zurab Tsereteli, Grant shows that this monument constructs and reveals a political imaginary that infantilizes public space and promotes an idea of historical innocence, meaning that the grandiosity of the statue helps contemporary Russians to identify with the projected glory of an imperial time, while skipping over the often painful Soviet past. **25** Tsereteli's statue represents Peter the Great as a larger-than-life conqueror of the seas who guides a gigantic ship. Sails and victory flags surrounding Peter's figure wave so exuberantly that—ironically—Peter himself seems to disappear. Considered one of Russia's most successful rulers, and the first ruler who took on the title of imperator, Peter seemingly represents the kind of strong leadership and stability that Russians began to long for during "the transition." In other words, the statue acts as a material sign of the desire for a supposedly simpler but also magnificent and regal past.

Monuments are deposits of memory. Yet although monuments, owing to their material quality, often appear fixed and stable, they do not contain memory in a stable form. This is not only because physical monuments are always subject to processes of destruction—for example, the physical processes of erosion and accretion—but also because the stories surrounding their production and meaning are variable and unsettled. For example, the fact that Tsereteli's statue is located in Moscow, a city that the historical Peter hated so much that he relocated Russia's capital from there to St. Petersburg, ironizes and undercuts the intended meaning of the statue. Likewise, other Tsereteli figures, such as the folkloric Russian bears, Ivan the Fool, and the Princess Frog in the neighborhood of Moscow's contemporary Manezh shopping mall are supposed to project serenity, harmony, and calm for a country at odds with itself. But their Disney-like disposition also marks them as kitsch: as monuments of comfort invested in historical innocence and positive feelings.

History on Trial

As the discussion above elucidates, within the context of the contemporary Russian Federation, memory tends to reveal itself as a tension-ridden, contradictory, paradoxical, and slippery practice. For example, during *perestroika* two bitterly opposed movements emerged, both of which carried the word *memory* in their names: Memorial and *Pamiat* ("Memory" in Russian). Founded in 1986, Memorial was created as an association of GULAG survivors and social support groups. Funded in part by the European Commission and the National Endowment for Democracy,

Figure 3.1 Young woman wearing a Soviet military cap in 2011.
Photo by the author

Memorial documents human rights abuses and the atrocities of the Stalinist past, and has established libraries and documentary archives in Moscow, St. Petersburg, and a number of other Russian cities and regional centers. To commemorate the victims of Stalinist terror, on October 30, 1990, Memorial placed a simple rock from the Solovetskii prison island in front of the Lubianka, the former headquarters of the KGB. In contradistinction, *Pamiat* is the name of a right-wing movement that at the end of the 1980s emerged in negative reaction to *glasnost* revelations about the Stalinist past, lamenting the destruction of Russian political culture. In tapping into a populist sense of resentment and humiliated national pride (see also Chapter 4), *Pamiat* has propagated a mythical worldview, blaming a Jewish and Masonic conspiracy for both Soviet and post-Soviet ills. While *Pamiat* disintegrated in the 1990s, many of its ideas had begun to infiltrate the mainstream, finding some outlets in Russian right-wing and nationalist movements (see Chapter 8).

The question of how Russia should deal with its difficult and violent past has occupied Russians since Mikhail Gorbachev's policy of *glasnost*. At stake in these debates—whether to remember or forget the past, when to address it, who should do it and how, and what its general relevance is today—is the content of school and university curricula, the celebration of public holidays, and the creation of a memetic culture (Smith 2002). As representations of history are being mulled over, and branded and re-branded, according to Alexander Etkind (2013) in the Russian Federation memory remains contested and essentially "at war."

In Russia, the question of how to deal with the Soviet past articulates itself most sharply in relation to the Stalinist past. From the mid-1920s

Figure 3.2 Russians posing with Lenin and Stalin in 2008. The boy wears a Young Pioneers scarf.

Photo by Justin Armstrong

to his death in 1953 Iosif Vissarionovich Dzhugashvili (1878–1953), better known as Stalin, was the leader of the Soviet Union. Following the death of Vladimir Lenin in 1924, Stalin began to consolidate his power. In the late 1920s he replaced the New Economic Policy (NEP)—a market-oriented economic policy deemed necessary after the 1922 end of the civil war—with a highly centralized command economy to launch collectivization and industrialization. These economic changes overlapped with the creation of the GULAG (*glavnoe upravlenie lagerei,* main administration of the camps), a network of labor camps in which by conservative estimates between 1929 and 1953 approximately 25 million people disappeared. Russia's White Sea-Baltic Canal, which connects the White Sea in the Arctic Ocean with Lake Onega, which is connected to the Baltic Sea, and some of today's northern Russian cities, including Vorkuta and Magadan, were built by GULAG prisoners. From 1936–38 Russia was seized by the Great Purges or the Great Terror (*bol'shoi terror*), Stalin's campaign of political repression, involving a large-scale purge of the Communist Party from so-called hostile elements, the repression of peasants, and widespread governmental surveillance and executions. A key feature of the Great Terror were the "Great Trials" in which the culpability of the defendants was already predetermined. Although in 1956 in a "secret speech" then-Party leader Nikita Khrushchev denounced Stalin's cult of personality, and although during the era of *glasnost* former prisoners published a number of important memoirs, to a significant part of the Russian population Stalin remains the "father of communism" (*zodchii kommunizma*) or "wise father" (*mudryi otets*). By contrast, to a liberal Russian public it can seem as if in public discourse Stalin's atrocities have been barely acknowledged.

Ethnographic Close-Up. Between August 2006 and July 2010, together with Justin Armstrong, I took a series of photographs of Russian and non-Russian families, women and men who themselves were having their picture taken with a doppelgänger of Stalin. We took most of these images in the vicinity of Moscow's Red Square, where Stalin's double tended to appear in the military garb of the exalted leader or *velikii vozhd'*. Carrying a Soviet flag he showed power (*moshch'*); smoking a pipe he projected simplicity and popular essence (*narodnost'*). As people lined up to have their picture taken with Stalin, they arranged themselves in ways that would always position Stalin in the photograph's center. Not only did those who appeared in the same frame as Stalin ask him to conspicuously show off the Soviet Union's flag, projecting power and coherence, but they also tended to stay close to him, as if to symbolize their admiration.

In those years, the amateur actors who doubled for Stalin were not the only reminder that Stalin's ghost continued to haunt the contemporary Russian Federation. Even just by throwing a passing glimpse at the items sold in Moscow in the Historical Museum's tourist shop or by street vendors on the city's Theater Square, one could see porcelain and stone figurines sculptured in Stalin's likeness, as well as cups, tea glasses, plates, and Matryoshka dolls imprinted with his portrait. Strolling a bit farther up one of Moscow's thoroughfares, *Okhotnoi Riad*, and taking a quick peek into the House of Books (*dom knigi*), one could see stamps featuring portraits of Stalin, and pins, posters, and banners demonstrating his glory. One was also able to buy an excellent reproduction of James Abbe's famous photograph of Stalin, showing him at a desk seated directly under a clearly visible portrait of Marx, or a miniature sculpture featuring Stalin together with Franklin D. Roosevelt and Winston Churchill at their historical April 1945 meeting in Yalta. In fact, in looking at these items typical of Russian souvenir culture, at times it seemed that the only artifacts that did not carry an image of Stalin were Russia's famous Palekh lacquer boxes and Dymkovo toys. But then, as Jan Plamber (2004) has remarked, the latter would not bear Stalin's likeness because of their largely Russian Orthodox and folk aesthetic connotations.

How should anthropologists make sense of the ways in which Stalin's ghost haunts contemporary Russia? In their descriptions of how in contemporary Russia positive recollections of the Stalinist past stay alive, both Margaret Paxson (2005) and Serguei Oushakine (2009) have chosen an emic approach, meaning that they explain Russia's sometimes less-than-critical approach to her past from a cultural and local perspective. For example, Paxson reports that in the village of Solovyovo where she conducted research in the 1990s, villagers continued to be invested in an almost mythic version of Stalin because in World War II he had led Russia to military victory and glory, and because—by extension—he was symbolically imbued with the power to take care of the many problems that had beset Russia in the 1990s. Similarly, Oushakine has documented how in the same period in the city of Barnaul Stalin remained a spectral presence because in people's understanding he appeared to be capable of healing the many political and emotional wounds—organized crime, widespread corruption, and spiraling inflation—that had begun to fester in Russia. Both anthropologists report that in the 1990s, following on the heels of the sheer endless revelations of *glasnost*, people had tired of what they had come to experience as that era's self-punishing political culture of historical introspection, fearing that Russia's critical remembering of the Stalinist past would open old wounds and tear Russia apart.

The question of how societies should deal with their difficult pasts is not easily answered. As countries across the world, including Chile, Argentina, Guatemala, Cambodia, South Africa, Rwanda, Germany, Russia, and the post-communist states of Central and Eastern Europe have started to confront their often violent histories, they have also developed a number of different approaches. TV series, public debates, new laws, and revised curricula have been among those strategies that continuously seek to address past wrongs on an ongoing basis, while the Truth and Reconciliation Commissions that have been established in some countries—although not in Russia—have labored hard to produce public consciousness and recognition of a nation's violent past. In Russia it is certainly the above-mentioned organization Memorial that remains most dedicated to the commemoration of the victims of Stalinist violence, although official and public support for such initiatives remains fickle. While Memorial has collected a formidable archive of oral testimonies, personal letters, and photographs, and even supported living victims, its offices have also been raided and electronic data from its archive seized. In November 2015 Russia's Justice Ministry marked Memorial as a "foreign agent" (see also Chapter 5). Similarly, Moscow's 2015 Victory Day parade, which featured tens of thousands of military servicemen and an ostentatious display of tanks, helicopters, and planes to celebrate the sixtieth anniversary of the Great Patriotic War, threw into relief the tensions that exist between those who demand a critical unearthing of the past and those who want to forget.

Religion

In his ethnography of the small town of Sepych in the Urals' upper Kama region, Douglas Rogers (2009) discusses how religious dissenters known as Old Believers have over the past three centuries sought to maintain their community and themselves by adapting and reconstructing their religious traditions. In the Russian context Old Believers form communities that emerged in the seventeenth century after the Russian Orthodox Church split into an official church and the Old Believers movement. At stake in this schism (*raskol*) were organizational questions—should Christian doctrine be carried out in a centralized church?—and orthographic reforms—for example, crossing one's self with two fingers instead of three, or debating the correct spelling of Jesus's name. Although from a contemporary perspective these may appear to be arcane questions, for Old Believers the anticipated reforms represented a moral threat to the central tenets of Christianity. Expelled from mainstream Russian Orthodoxy, Old Believers began to flee persecution and settled in rather remote areas of Imperial Russia.

In contrast to popular histories and imaginations that depict Old Believers as inflexible, doctrinaire, and pedantic devotees, Rogers argues that Sepych's Old Believers do not treat their beliefs as dogma, but rather invent and construct these to sustain themselves throughout time. In adopting a temporal frame that spans three centuries and focuses on the periods that followed significant historical upheavals—the emancipation of Russian serfs in 1861, the socialist period, and post-socialism—Rogers shows how Sepych Old Believers have survived by continuously adopting a conscious orientation toward what is virtuous, doable, proper, or good. For example, in discussing how the community managed to sustain itself in the supposedly agnostic socialist period, Rogers explores how Sepych practices of deferring ritual participation until later in life allowed Old Believers to be active in the community's collective farm without abandoning their beliefs. At the same time, religious practices changed as Old Believers, for example, chose baptism in churches run by priests, rather than in priestless Old Believer communities. As the protection associated with baptism—from disease, physical ailments, or early death—took dominance over religious affiliation, people began to prefer more authoritative and supposedly efficient modes of religious practice over the less orchestrated Old Believer baptismal rituals. Rather than basing religious and ethical decisions on Old Believer doctrine, they based them on their changing understandings of what felt right and good.

The question of what is ethical, moral, and right also drives Jarret Zigon's (2011) analysis of Russian Orthodox Church (ROC)-run rehabilitation programs for intravenous drug users. However, instead of focusing on issues of social change, he situates his analysis of the church's therapeutic process on moral personhood: What does it mean to be a good and "normal" person? In concretely examining the church-run rehabilitation program at the Mill, a ROC facility close to St. Petersburg, Zigon describes how religious–therapeutic techniques such as prayer, confession, penance, and taking responsibility for one's self are based on Christian assumptions that one is born a sinner, and thus one must continuously struggle and work to be a good person. Religious–therapeutic techniques, intimately tied to Orthodox notions of morality, human rights, and personhood, are thus important tools for disciplining the self. For example, in recounting the bodily sensations of various subjects who have decided to take part in the Mill's rehabilitation program Zigon describes how prayer quiets emotional turbulences, making subjects feel more at ease and at peace with themselves.

Albeit in a very different vein than the one suggested by Zigon, in her analysis of the complex relationship between politics and religion Anya Bernstein (2013a) also considers the techniques of the senses and the body. For example, in describing *chöd*, a Buddhist ritual with a long and complex history and lineage, Bernstein asks about its current significance in post-socialist times, especially for women. *Chöd*, which tends to be translated as "cutting off," is a Tibetan meditative technique for cutting attachment to the ego through the central practice of offering one's body as food to various extra-human agents, including boddhisattvas, spirits, gods, and demons. As Bernstein describes it, it involves a tantric technique of consciousness transfer: ejecting one's consciousness from one's body. While there exist many forms of consciousness transfer, one employed at the time of Bernstein's fieldwork involved a technique in which one had to visualize one's consciousness in one's heart in the form of Vajravarahi, a wrathful form of the Buddhist goddess Vajrayogini, and then make it fly up one's central channel and shoot out through the so-called Brahma aperture on the top of one's head. As soon as consciousness exits the body, the body becomes a corpse and collapses in a heap. As the *chöd* practitioner, now in the form of Vajravarahi, sees the lifeless corpse lying on the ground, he or she starts to dismember it with a cleaver, separating different body parts according to specific instructions given in the ritual text. One's body parts are then offered to different spirits and demons to either appease or satisfy them.

One of the questions that interests Bernstein within the context of *chöd* is why so many women are drawn to this particular ritual. As she argues, especially in light of the fairly high status of women in the Soviet Union, post-socialist Buryatia (among other places) seems to have undergone a re-traditionalization of **gender** roles (see Chapter 6), which has resulted in an increasingly masculine interpretation of Buddhism, including the exclusion of women from many rituals. Denied official roles in Buddhist establishments, and with no institutional structures for female Buddhist education, Buryat women thus resort to lay religious practices, or non-clerical tantric practices like *chöd*. Thus, it is not only the fact that *chöd* was founded by a female saint with whom many Buddhist women identify, or that *chöd* suits women because one visualizes oneself as a female deity, or because women are more naturally given to "giving," but also because the ritual assists them in asserting themselves as more powerful, as being endowed with more spiritual connections and dignity, than institutional-ized Buddhist frameworks in contemporary Russia allow.

Suggested Discussion Questions

Why and how did Russian citizens experience the demise of the Soviet Union in terms of loss? Why did they feel nostalgic? What do those feelings indicate? What constitutes the significance of the Stalinist past for contemporary Russia? And how has religion become an indicator of social and cultural change in Russia?

Suggestions for Further Reading

Aitamurto, Kaarina. 2016. *Paganism, Traditionalism, Nationalism: Narratives of Russian "Rodnoverie."* London: Routledge.

Goluboff, Sascha. 2003. *Jewish Russians: Upheavals in a Moscow Synagogue.* Philadelphia: University of Pennsylvania Press. https://doi.org/10.9783/9780812202038.

Kotkin, Stephen. 1995. *Magnetic Mountain: Stalinism as a Civilization.* Berkeley: University of California Press.

Luehrmann, Sonja. 2011. *Secularism Soviet Style: Teaching Atheism and Religion in a Volga Republic*. Bloomington: Indiana University Press.

—. 2015. *Religion in Secular Archives: Soviet Atheism and Historical Knowledge*. Oxford: Oxford University Press. https://doi.org/10.1093/acprof:oso/9780199943623.001.0001.

Paperno, Irina. 2009. *Stories of the Soviet Experience: Memoirs, Diaries, Dreams*. Ithaca, NY: Cornell University Press. https://doi.org/10.7591/9780801459115.

Plamper, Jan. 2012. *The Stalin Cult: A Study in the Alchemy of Power*. New Haven: Yale University Press.

Scheffel, David. 1991. *In the Shadow of Anti-Christ: The Old Believers of Alberta*. Toronto: University of Toronto Press.

Steinberg, Mark D., and Catherine Wanner, eds. 2008. *Religion, Morality, and Community in Post-Soviet Societies*. Bloomington: Indiana University Press.

Wanner, Catherine. 2007. *Communities of the Converted: Ukrainians and Global Evangelism*. Ithaca, NY: Cornell University Press.

33

CHAPTER 4

IDENTITY, NATIONALISM, AND COMMUNITY-MAKING

In December 1991 the socialist and multinational Soviet Union disintegrated into 15 separate states: Kazakhstan, Kyrgyzstan, Tajikistan, Turkmenistan, Uzbekistan, Armenia, Georgia, Azerbaijan, Belarus, Moldova, Ukraine, Estonia, Latvia, Lithuania, and Russia. The violent conflicts in the late 1980s in the Caucasus, Ukraine, and Baltic regions not only exposed Soviet state-sponsored discourses of the coherence of the *sovetskii narod* (Soviet people) as myths, but also began to lay bare a number of problematic political and national assumptions. Among these were suppositions that the socialist cause had outplayed national loyalties and identifications (Suny 1993) and that *sliianie*, the merging of peoples, had been an unqualified success. As a variety of ethnographic studies—ranging from Alaina Lemon's (2000) study of Romani stereotyping and exclusion, to Greta Uehling's (2004) research on the cultural memory and national repatriation movement of Crimean Tatars, to David Anderson's (2000) work on Evenki reindeer herders' sense of belonging, to Marjorie Mandelstam Balzer's (1999) examination of Khanty cultural activism—show, in the aftermath of the Soviet Union's collapse, questions of cultural and collective **identity** assumed massive significance.

In the anthropology of Russia (as elsewhere), identity is a broad term, encompassing dynamics of sameness and difference, exclusion and inclusion, conflict, power, ideology, and belonging. In other words, identity denotes the ways in which we understand ourselves and others by sharing certain characteristics or by negating and disavowing them. As a form of self-identification, identity can refer to individuals ("I am Russian"), nations and communities ("Russians don't like to be stereotyped"), or even collectives

("The Soviet collective will build the future"). In general, analysts differentiate between the terms *communities* and *collectives* by suggesting that the word "communities" indexes a more seamless and tradition-oriented whole, while collectives are more self-conscious and loose, less shaped by a sense of tradition, and more oriented to the future.

In Russia, one of the principal ways of defining identity has been through the idea of the **nation**. As Rogers Brubaker (1996) has argued, from a political perspective the nation is an organizing principle of political space. Although nations are often understood as real entities—as primordial, substantial, and enduring groups—as a concept the nation tends to hover between two mutually antagonistic approaches. Posited as an essentialist idea, the nation is marked by a fundamentally unchanging core of meaning that precedes and transcends culture and politics. Here national identity derives its sense and legitimacy from its supposed grounding in nature and/or history, where "history" is seen as a linear and unbroken line of development. By contrast, **constructivist** approaches tend to emphasize the historical, cultural, and political circumstances in which national identities are produced. Largely building on Benedict Anderson's ([1983] 1991) book entitled *Imagined Communities: Reflections on the Origin and Spread of Nationalism*, in contemporary and anthropological discourses of Russia social constructivists (Hirsch 2005; Martin 2001; Slezkine 1994) argue that "the nation" always takes shape in particular historical, economic, and political circumstances.

In this chapter my underlying concern is with looking at the ways in which the anthropology of Russia has examined various national identity formations. I begin by outlining one of the most complex and vexing questions facing analysts of Russia today: how to define the meanings of "being Russian." As the discussion will show, principally, two approaches have emerged. The first one stresses Russia's supposed need for marking itself as the "core nation" of the *multinational* Russian Federation. A "core nation" is a nation that understands itself in primordial terms, and as central to a given polity. **Nationalism**, by extension, describes a mode of identification in which political claims are made in the name of a "core nation." The second argues that there exists no such thing as an essential Russian-ness. Rather, self-understandings of "being Russian" emerge out of a complex web of cultural meanings, of which cultural symbols and stories are a significant part. These approaches can appear as disparate and even contradictory, but they come together in problematizing the idea of Russian culture as "always already there" by throwing into relief questions about the national uses of Russian-ness.

Building on Julie Hemment's (2015) study of Kremlin-sponsored and nationalist youth projects in Russia, in the second part I delineate how Russian nationalism is not always already authoritarian and "strong," but continuously needs to reproduce itself to strengthen the idea of the nation. In the example that I cite, "reproduction" consists of educational and entrepreneurial interaction aimed specifically at Russia's youth. While keeping the politics of Russian "nation-ness" in mind, in the third part I turn my attention to the cultural rights struggles of Russia's indigenous communities. As I have mentioned before, in the era of *perestroika* in Russia the cultural rights struggle began to explode, and—eventually—contributed to the demise of the Soviet Union. In building on my own research with indigenous rights activists in the Chukotka Peninsula in the Russian Far East (Rethmann 2004), I emphasize the contradictory legacies of the Soviet Union's unique policies to ethnic pluralism, especially as they pivot on the institutionalization of multinationality.

Russia and the Nation

Within the context of the contemporary Russian Federation, discussions revolving around issues of cultural identity and difference tend to be tense, contradictory, and complex. In the years after the collapse of the Soviet Union one of the most critical tasks facing the Russian Federation was not merely the invention of new political structures, but also the forging of new identities from the remains of a multinational state marked by its own structures of cohesion, hierarchy, and inequality. Below I briefly outline some of the ways in which, in Russia, discussions about what it means to be Russian articulate themselves.

In the era of the Soviet Union, Russian was, of course, the dominant ethnicity and state language of the Soviet empire. Its federation was the largest in the Soviet Union, and its capital clock marked the country's state time. However, in the Soviet era Russians were not permitted their own institutions, including their own radio, television programming, news agency, Communist Party, or even secret police (KGB). Although Russian ethnic pride was thoroughly—if inconsistently—marked as Soviet pride, Russians tended to bemoan the fact that their own ethnicity was left unspecified, drained by the homogenizing notion of "the Soviet people." According to anthropologist Ernest Gellner (1990), it is in this curious back and forth between hyper-recognition and non-recognition that Russian desires for a "robust nation" are to be found.

Although the idea that Russia should be considered a nation-state has been enjoying some popularity since *perestroika*—but also before—it flies in the face of the fact that in 1993 the Russian Federation was declared to be a multinational federation. The fact that the Russian Federation does not cohere as a nation is also evinced by the linguistic distinction between two words for "Russian," *rossiiskii* and *russkii*. As *rossiiskii*, Russia is not marked as a nation-state but as a pluralistic state that also gestures at its imperial history. As *russkii*, "Russia" does not constitute a nation-state but an ethnicity. There exist no official documents that explicitly call ethnic Russians a "state-bearing" people; instead, officially the government supports a civic or *rossiiskaia* identity that encompasses Russians along with other nationalities. In contemporary Russia, then, national identity should not be considered a natural, essentialist, or primordial category, but a process or project whose invocation is never without political elements and repercussions.

The Robust Nation

As Serguei Oushakine (2009) has shown, in the mid-1990s Russia one particularly powerful cultural imagination emerged that did conceive of ethnicity as more or less naturally determined—instead of, as abovementioned Western colleagues like Ernest Gellner (1990) and Benedict Anderson ([1983] 1991) argued, historically or culturally constructed. Extensively discussed by ethnographer Lev Nikolaevich Gumilev (1912–92), the son of poets Anna Akhmatova and Nikolai Gumilev and a victim of Stalin's repressive politics, this imagination is based on chauvinistic conceptualizations of geography and soil, and—to some extent—purity of blood (Bassin 2017). Although Gumilev's ideas are complex, he argues that each ethnic or national group (*etnos*) constitutes a biological and homogenous organism that evinces its own inherited racial-biological characteristics. The health of each *etnos* originates from and is developed in a particular physiological environment, and its healthy existence depends on maintaining that environment. Consequently, Gumilev also takes a rather uncompromising stand against *sliianie* and/or ethnic hybridity. While, perhaps contradictorily, Gumilev also developed the idea of a "superethnos" that would bring together different nationalities in harmony, right-wing segments of Russia's population build on Gumilev's ideas to argue for the necessity of a certain purity in national culture.

The Constructed Nation

In her book *Russia and Soul* Dale Pesmen (2000) pursues a different approach to understanding what it means to "be Russian." Building on the Russian philosopher, literary critic, and semiotician Mikhail Bakhtin's (1981) concept of heteroglossia (*raznorechie*), which delineates the existence of various voices within a single language or "tongue," Pesmen shows that the Russian notion of "soul" (*dusha*) does not constitute an essentialist whole but is rather a layered, fragmented, inchoate, and inherently slippery concept. In chronicling everyday cultural practices such as mushroom gathering, shopping, and drinking, as well as the stories Russians tell about these practices, she illustrates how "Russian-ness" emerges in the interplay of different cultural practices, rhetorics, values, and voices.

Although Pesmen argues that *dusha* is a complex and multilayered concept, she also recognizes that "soul" finds some of its most political resonances in Russian nationalist thought. For example, in looking at the ways in which nineteenth-century novelists and philosophers talked about *dusha* in order to distinguish themselves from the West's supposed lack of soul—its emphasis on rationality, precision, and reserve, and culture of predictability and calculation—she cites Petr Chaadaev's 1836 publication *Philosophical Letters*, in which the author describes the splitting of Russia's intellectuals into two camps, Westernizers and Slavophiles. Westernizers believed that Russia was more backward than Europe and welcomed, for example, Peter the Great's Enlightenment ambitions. Slavophiles tended to be set against many of the changes associated with the Enlightenment and the West, condemning them for betraying Russia's unique virtues, including *sobornost'* or social collectivity, which made Russia superior and not inferior to the individualistic West. As should be clear from the discussions above, these antagonisms are, of course, not relegated to the past but continue to exist today.

39

Nationalism and Entrepreneurship

In her study of nationalist youth projects Julie Hemment (2015), too, argues that the nation does not constitute a culturally self-evident and automatic form of identification, but—rather—that the emotional and affective ties that sustain it need to be continuously reproduced. In focusing in particular on the high-profile Seliger educational youth camp that took place in 2009 at a popular resort lake in the region of Tver', she examines how the Kremlin-sponsored and nationalist youth movement *nashi* (ours) does not employ always already authoritarian forms of nationalism to forge attachments to the nation, but rather relies on "soft" means—such as offering educational and entrepreneurial assistance to Russia's youth—and thus struggles to stay competitive in the Russian and global labor market. For example, in 2009 the Seliger camp ran eight themed sessions—leadership, entrepreneurship (two sessions), tolerance, voluntarism, tourism, public relations, and art—each of which centered on business-related values: learning financial and business planning, creating sellable products, carving out a competitive advantage, and forging commercial connections. In channeling attachments to the nation through the promise of entrepreneurial success, Kremlin-sponsored and *nashi* facilitators build on positive emotions such as confidence and gratitude to frame nationalist values as affirmative of one's self and Russia—and not as always already hateful propaganda.

Indigenous Rights Struggles in Russia

Deriving from the Latin term *indigenus*, which roughly translates as "born or produced from within," the word "indigenous" suggests nativeness, originating from within a particular place and/or country, "being deeply rooted in one place." At stake in its definition are conditions of temporal priority, histories of colonialism, and demands for inclusion and rights. In specific relation to Russia, the term "indigenous peoples" (*korennye narodnosti*) is most often applied to the *malochislennye* (small in number) peoples of Siberia, the Russian North, and the Russian Far East, although it also refers to Old Believer, Mennonite, and other non-Russian Orthodox Church communities. What's more, in the contemporary Russian polity the term has become highly contested, especially as it relates to struggles over rights, governance, and land.

40

As anthropologists (Grant 1995; Trouillot 2004; Anderson 2000) have shown, as non-European and radical others, in Russia—and elsewhere—indigenous peoples tend to be associated with tropes of backwardness. In other words, they tend to be considered less cultured, enlightened, developed, or civilized. For example, the fact that traditionally the majority of Russia's indigenous peoples are not settled but herd reindeer while they migrate across a vast expanse of tundras and taigas can be seen as a sign of primitivity. The same holds true for the fact that whaling, walrus and seal hunting, fishing, and collecting mussels, seaweed, birds' eggs, and various kinds of berries and tundra herbs also constitute meaningful ways of making a living. By extension, animals and plants endow indigenous peoples with a deep sense of who they are, and it is this identity that forms the basis for many indigenous rights politics and struggles.

In the example below I discuss some of the challenges and possibilities for indigenous rights organizing in contemporary Russia, especially as it emerged at the beginning of this century. In the 1990s and in 2000 I spent a great deal of time working with the indigenous residents of the Russian Far East, assisting them—among other things—to garner funding for some of their own political projects. In describing a tradition-centered attempt at indigenous self-empowerment below, I highlight some of the conditions necessary for indigenous identity to flourish, and also emphasize the Soviet and contemporary Russian understandings of identity that indigenous activists feel they are up against. The Soviet Union's own unique approach to ethnic pluralism, especially in the form of institutionalized nationhood, plays a significant role here, as do indigenous struggles with its contradictory and paradoxical legacies.

To outsiders, the fairly high status and power indigenous representatives can enjoy at state levels in the Soviet Union might be surprising, but—as Rogers Brubaker (1996) and in particular Terry Martin (2001) have shown—the "affirmative action empire" was the Soviet Union's own unique response to a problem that troubles most multinational states: how to integrate cultural multiplicity within larger institutions by maintaining, at least in appearance, justice and equality among them. The answer to this question, the nation-builders, including Lenin, argued, lay in the implementation of affirmative action policies in the name of *korenizatsiia* or "indigenization." What this is usually taken to mean is that the Soviet state not only passively tolerated but actively institutionalized the existence of multiple nationalities as fundamental constituents of the state.

In the official language of the Soviet state, one of its key aims was appeasement and accommodation. In the 1920s, ritualized stagings of cultural life—dramatizations of "culture" in the form of theater, artistic movements, song, and dance—sprang up all across the Soviet Union. Following the Soviet creed that culture should be "nationalist in form, [but] socialist in content," the tradition of "the people" metamorphosed into fetishized articulations of the regime's good intentions and will. In the 1930s, in the name of "allying" (*smychka*) and the "Friendship of the Peoples" (*druzhba narodov*)—a catchphrase created to inspire a sense of cultural equality and social mutuality—policies were developed to bind the Soviet Union's various cultural constituencies. As already mentioned, in the mid-1980s the "Friendship of the Peoples" began to reveal itself as myth, and the Soviet Union's increasing fragmentation began to stand as a sign of how fragile and porous this "friendship" had always been.

A Very Brief History of Indigenous Organizing in Russia, through the Particular Lens of Chukotka

In March 1990 a number of prominent indigenous activists and writers created the Association of the Indigenous Minorities of the Far North, Siberia, and the Far East. Initially, the association listed 26 cultural groups that would exist under its auspices. In November 1993 the association morphed into the Russian Association of the Indigenous Peoples of the North (RAIPON), which now functions as an umbrella organization for 35 indigenous and ethnic organizations. The purpose of RAIPON is to (1) create regional and local venues for an indigenous voice, (2) channel information concerning indigenous issues and rights into villages and regions, (3) dispense monetary aid and funding for indigenous projects, and (4) guarantee the flow of knowledge and advice between Moscow and the regions, and among the regions. Organizationally, RAIPON works with the State Duma and the Government of the Russian Federation on issues related to indigenous legislation. It also forms an integral part of international political bodies such as the Arctic Council and the United Nations Permanent Forum on Indigenous Issues.

While on a national level RAIPON is certainly the most significant indigenous organization in Russia, in regional and local contexts its politics are not always undisputed. For example, when in the first decade of this century I conducted some *applied anthropology*—by which anthropologists mean the application of the methods and theories of anthropology to the analysis and solution of practical problems—in Chukotka, I assisted an indigenous movement by the name of Ionto to raise some funding. Ionto consisted of an eclectic mix of Chukchi, Even, and Evenk indigenous elders, and young and independent leaders, and was created to expand the possibilities for indigenous self-organizing in the region. In seeking ways to imagine political initiatives in cultural terms, Ionto's members built on historical, cultural, and political traditions to envision community-oriented modes of organizing. Concretely, in the early 2000s the movement sought to revive the idea of historical trade fairs as a significant site of economic and cultural exchange (Rethmann 2004). Specifically, one of its initiators, Anton Tynel', saw the fairs as the basis for a particular form of trade activism, meaning that people would no longer be dependent on government hand-outs but would be able to set the conditions for their own empowerment. This is what Anton said: "The fair is the foundation of our independence. If we start now, in the beginning, only two or three people will come. Let them bring meat, and nothing more; let them bring animal hides, and nothing more. But this will be the beginning of our trade activism. We will do it ourselves and not through some government. That is what we will do for ourselves, we will do it for a long time" (Rethmann 2004: 264).

A Brief Glimpse of Chukchi History and Identity

In Chukchi communities, people remember trade fairs and the mobility associated with them as important and constitutive aspects of their livelihood. In Chukchi memory, trade fairs—dense networks of economic transaction and exchange—were important places of *biznis* and commerce, connecting different indigenous communities—Chukchi, Koriak, Even, Inupiat—and non-indigenous communities—Russian, Japanese, and American—into a single marketplace. Trade fairs entered the ethnographic record as early as 1789 (Bogoraz 1904), and were then held in the Chukotka Peninsula in the area of Ostrovnye and Anui at irregular intervals. Eventually the latter location prevailed and Fort Anuisk was built. The Anui fair grew rapidly in importance. Elders confirm that there must have been fairs in remote villages to which people traveled, offering their wares. Their mobility and autonomy allowed Chukchi herders to establish far-reaching trade relations in the region, and stretch out—across the ocean—throughout the entire Bering region.

Historic change at the turn of the century, however, forced Chukchi traders to shift the emphasis in trade from intraregional to interregional relations, resulting in the intensification of trade among Chukotka's indigenous and non-indigenous constituencies. When I lived in the Peninsula, Chukchi elders recalled some of the specificities of such exchanges in great detail, and cultural memories of this trade continue to mobilize younger Chukchi as sites of meaningful action, enabling communication between generations. Younger people ask about the prizes for knives and rifles (how many reindeer hides did you sell to buy a gun?), and older people consult each other and their memory to answer these questions as accurately as they can. To the Chukchi women and men I knew, interregional trade identified them as wide-traveling and knowledgeable: trading people were people who could manage their own affairs.

In fashioning its own vision of autonomy, Ionto worked hard to create political meanings that might resonate with all Chukchi and other indigenous peoples the movement's activists know. Anton's statement was not a statement that addressed the political desires and hopes of Chukchi women **43** and men in the name of transcendent abstractions: justice, democracy, sustainability, and human rights. It was precisely because the statement deployed Chukchi history, memory, and knowledge to inspire indigenous women and men that Ionto was able to create promising openings for activist mobilization. In 1998 Chukchi activists from the western Chukotka territory of Bilibino organized such a fair to protest against the radiation and emissions from Bilibino's nuclear power station, which had killed animals, humans, and plants. To the excitement of everybody involved, the idea was a success. Bilibino's resident Chukchi were there, but many more arrived from far away to participate. A historical and tradition-oriented space had been created and cleared within a political landscape not always conducive to granting Chukchi women and men agency within the imaginations of their own making.

Soviet Paradoxes and Legacies of Nation-building
As I've mentioned before, at the beginning of the 1920s Soviet officials began to devise a set of national policies marked by local—if limited—self-rule. Specifically Soviet theorists of nationality thought that they could undermine the allure of nationalism by granting a form of territorial nationhood to a number of definable national groups. As both Kate Brown (2015) and Terry Martin (2001) have argued, at the time the Soviet experiment was one of the most progressive nationality policies in the European world. Rather than simply subjugating national minorities to the cultural domination of the majority, as in tsarist Russia, the Soviet state promoted and sponsored local councils, courts, newspapers, schools, clubs, Communist Party cells, and, when populations were sufficiently large to warrant it, entire regional governments for each national minority, all to be run in that minority's language. In 1930, the Soviet government created the Chukotka National District.

In her work on cultural rights activism in Chukotka Patty Gray (2005) has described the complex ways in which Soviet affirmative action policies articulated themselves in the Chukotka region. In April 1932, roughly two years after the inception of the Chukotka National District, the First

Chukotka Okrug Congress of Soviets decided to inaugurate a parallel political system by which to grant both indigenous and non-indigenous Communist Party members equity and politically balanced shares of power. In the beginning of the 1990s, the chairperson of Chukotka's Soviet of Workers' Deputies was Russian, while the chairperson of the Soviet's Executive Committee was indigenous. In a highly formalistic implementation of this rule, from 1932 until 1991, Chukchi women or men served as chairpersons of the region's Executive Committee. To the astonishment of Chukotka's residents, this rule was reversed when in 1991 Chukchi politician Vladimir Mikhailovich Etylin was elected chairperson of the Soviet of Worker's Deputies, while a Russian "newcomer," Aleksandr Viktorovich Nazarov, was chosen as chairperson of the Executive Committee.

In the eyes of many Chukchi women and men, the termination of *korenizatsiia* in 1991 ended 70 years of affirmative action and greatly distressed Chukotka's indigenous residents since it effectively started to bar them from governmental positions of decision-making. Aleksandr Nazarov, who, after Yeltsin's 1993 dissolution of all Soviets of Workers' Deputies, speedily advanced to the position of governor, ruled by harassment, intimidation, and authoritarian decree. Departmental divisions that dealt exclusively with indigenous affairs were closed. In 1996 the *iaranga* (Chukchi term for the traditional reindeer-fur-covered tent that was used by reindeer-herding Chukchi), a meeting place for various Chukchi cultural and political groups, was disbanded, and in the same year the indigenous and independent newspaper, *Murgin Nutenut* (Our Homeland), was terminated. Indigenous demonstrations and public protests led to manifold dismissals of Chukchi government officials. Demands for new movements and institutions that would no longer mirror Soviet bureaucratic understandings appeared. Traditionally self-conscious indigenous activists began to challenge governmental policies and thus to create a political space in which indigenous issues could be heard.

Challenges to Cultural Recognition and Pluralism

The ideals of the Soviet Union may be gone, but its legacy lives on. In the beginning of this century in the Chukotka Autonomous Region this was nowhere more evident than in the ritualized forms of public recognition, including recognition of cultural difference and rights. On August 9, 2000, the new democratic government of Chukotka celebrated the "International Day of Indigenous Peoples," in Anadyr. The celebration, conducted under the auspices of the regional government, assumed a grandly theatrical form. In keeping with the theme of the day, the elevated stage engulfed almost one-third of the plaza that stretched out in front of Anadyr's House of Culture (*dom kul'tury*), with the municipal administration doing its best to approximate some sort of original Chukchi culture. Indeed, there was nothing particularly spectacular in Anadyr's rendition. An open and wide *iaranga*, with all the trappings of typical Chukchi life, furnished the background and the illusion of cultural simplicity and authenticity. Reindeer-hide-covered drums were hanging from cords along the side of the tent. Boots, mattresses, and coats sewn from reindeer fur lay on the ground, and simulations of Chukchi petroglyphic imagery of sea mammals, including whales and seals, as well as boats and hunting scenes, had been painted on pieces of cardboard, each of which was attached to the stage. Antlers, bows, and the odd spear stuck out everywhere, and a rounded plate representing the sun as one quintessential Chukchi sign of life, shone over the scene. **45**

Under the slogan "our way, our pride," difference, not collectivity, took center stage. Governor Aleksandr Nazarov spoke of educational achievements, justice, and of debt: "Ahead of us there is a task. Together with preservation of the ethnic and cultural uniqueness of the indigenous peoples of the North, we will also need to elevate them to the level of a modern civilization. Our debt today: the continuous, harmonious and, most importantly, compassionate introduction of our indigenous peoples to a modern level of life." Others, too, spoke in enthusiastic, albeit very general, ways of the accomplishments and kindheartedness of the governor. The Chukchi that I knew who were present observed this newly democratic but also terribly chauvinistic scene with their own air of practiced attachment.

It will be remembered that in the political culture of the Soviet Union the recognition of Russia's non-Russian constituencies was situated at the threshold between negation and affirmation, between the denial of culture as a site of difference and its avowal as folkloric aestheticization. This was a dialectics that created its own particular form of exclusion by purportedly empowering that which it sought to keep out of its political realm. As Chukchi women and men were well aware, the logics of this system had not been abandoned but lived on—in the creation of new political vocabularies and legal language, rhetorics of patronage masquerading as kindness, dependencies disguised as guardianship. No one other than the governor made this clearer. On that day, in an act of magnanimous ostentation, Aleksandr Nazaroc had allowed himself the pleasure of a special gesture. Piles and piles of pinkish-gray layers of bowhead whale fat were heaped on long wooden boards outside the *iaranga*. The adjoining banner read: From the Governor.

Suggested Discussion Questions

Why is the issue of Russian identity so contentious in Russia? What does it mean to speak of cultural identity as constructed, instead of as essentialist? Why is national identity often perceived in essentialist terms? How are claims of indigenous identity situated in relation to claims of Russian identity?

Suggestions for Further Reading

Bassin, Mark, and Catriona Kelly, eds. 2012. *Soviet and Post-Soviet Identities*. Cambridge: Cambridge University Press. https://doi.org/10.1017/CBO9780511894732.

Bassin, Mark, and Ronald G. Suny, eds. 2016. *The Gumilev Mystique: Biopolitics, Eurasianism, and the Construction of Community in Modern Russia*. Ithaca, NY: Cornell University Press.

Brubaker, Rogers. 2006. *Ethnicity without Groups*. Cambridge, MA: Harvard University Press.

Condee, Nancy. 2009. *The Imperial Trace: Recent Russian Cinema*. Oxford: Oxford University Press. https://doi.org/10.1093/acprof:oso/9780195366761.001.0001.

Donahoe, Brian, and Joachim Otto Habeck, eds. 2011. *Reconstructing the House of Culture: Community, Self, and the Making of Culture in Russia and Beyond*. New York: Berghahn Books.

Fikes, Kesha, and Alaina Lemon. 2002. "African Presence in Former Soviet Spaces." *Annual Review of Anthropology* 31 (1): 497–524. https://doi.org/10.1146/annurev.anthro.31.040402.085420.

Kivelson, Valerie, and Ronald Suny. 2016. *Russia's Empires*. Oxford: Oxford University Press.

Shnirelman, Victor. 2009. "New Racism, 'Clash of Civilizations,' and Russia." In *Russian Nationalism and the National Reassertion of Russia*, edited by Marlene Laruelle, 125–44. New York: Routledge.

Slezkine, Yuri. 1994. *Arctic Mirrors: Russia and the Small Peoples of the North*. Ithaca, NY: Cornell University Press.

Suny, Ronald G. 1993. *The Revenge of the Past: Nationalism, Revolution, and the Collapse of the Soviet Union*. Stanford: Stanford University Press.

Tishkov, Valery, and Martha Brill Olcott. 1999. "From Ethnos to Demos: The Quest for Russia's Identity." In *Russia Transformed*, edited by Anders Aslund and Martha Brill Olcott, 61–90. Washington: Carnegie Endowment for International Peace.

CHAPTER 5

POLITICAL CULTURE, DEMOCRACY, AND PROTEST

Ethnographic Close-Up

On the morning of February 21, 2012, five young women entered the Cathedral of Christ the Savior in central Moscow to stage what they called a "punk prayer." Wearing multicolored stockings, neon-colored dresses, and balaclavas, they took out their guitars and began a song that was a cross between punk riffs and an Orthodox chant. Dancing on an elevated platform in front of the cathedral's altar, they kicked and boxed for the song's fast parts, and knelt and bowed for the song's liturgical parts. Chanting "Virgin Mary, Mother of God, chase Putin out, chase Putin out, chase Putin out," the song criticized the close relations between Putin and Patriarch Kirill (only a few days before, on February 8, Russian television had broadcast a conversation between Putin and Patriarch Kirill in which the latter described the flush 2000s as "God's miracle, greatly aided by the country's leadership"), and the Orthodox Church's conservative gender and anti-LGBTQ rhetoric. All of them were active members of Russia's all-female art collective and punk-rock band Pussy Riot.

Like all of Pussy Riot's performances—the band had staged previous ones in Moscow's Red Square and in Moscow's Cathedral of the Apparition—the one that took place in the Cathedral of Christ the Savior had been secretly planned, although it was supposed to be videotaped by a number of trusted documenters. Yet somehow news had leaked out; journalists were already waiting in the church when the women arrived. They nevertheless decided to go ahead with their *aktion* (action). But just a few bars into their song, one of the cathedral's security guards pulled the balaclava off one of the women's heads, exposing her face, even if only for a few minutes. The women fled, but on February 26, the day known in the Russian Orthodox tradition as Forgiveness Sunday, the Russian government filed charges against the five unnamed women. On March 3, less than two weeks after the event, three members—Nadezhda Tolokonnikova, Maria Alyokhina, and Ekaterina Samutsevich—were arrested.

Images of the trial that took place in the summer of 2012 in Moscow's Khamovnichesky Courthouse spread around the globe. The women were placed inside what Russians called "the aquarium": a Plexiglas enclosure equipped with microphones for the defendants to address the court and a small horizontal window so that they could pass papers back and forth to their defense attorneys. Only journalists were allowed to approach the courthouse, and only a few of them were able to fit into the overcrowded courtroom. Scholars (Schuler 2013) have described the trial as a "show trial"—that is, as a trial reminiscent of the Stalinist trials that between 1936 and 1938 took place in Soviet Russia to undermine governmental opposition and consolidate Joseph Stalin's regime, and in which the judicial authorities had already predetermined the defendants' guilt. On August 17, Tolokonnikova, Alyokhina, and Samutsevich were convicted of hooliganism, and on October 12 Tolokonnikova and Alyokhina were sent to separate prisons. Two days before, on October 10, Samutsevich was freed on probation, her sentence suspended. On December 23, 2013, after the State Duma had approved their amnesty, Tolokonnikova and Alyokhina were released from prison.

Taking this trial as a point of departure, in this chapter I look at some of the ways in which anthropologists have examined issues of political culture in Russia. By *political culture* I mean the ways in which people believe and understand politics: how they feel about it, how they experience power, and with what consequences. Political culture thus involves a number of institutional and agentive dimensions that do not always cohere. Building on the protest character of Pussy Riot's action, as well as the response of the state to its performance, I ask what kinds of political **agency** and protest have emerged in Russia. I examine how political activists seek to negotiate, challenge, or even resist the logic and structures of governmental and bureaucratic power, and I ask about the conditions that both enable and delimit Russian citizens' ability to build up meaningful forms of **democracy** and civil society. This chapter builds on the assumption that democracy in Russia is problematic and often takes illiberal forms, including curtailments of fair elections and the free press (see Chapter 7).

I begin this chapter by briefly providing a history of Vladimir Putin's presidency to set the context within which many of the forms of political agency and protest that I describe need to be seen. In Russia there exist a number of terms for state power—*derzhavnost'* as the condition of being a powerful geopolitical state that commands the attention and respect of other countries; *gosudarstvennichestvo* as administrative and law-making power; *pravitel'stvo* as governing power; *vlast'* as pure, raw power; and *sila* as physical strength—all of which come together in understandings of the state as solid and strong. In my discussion of Putin's governance, I focus more on the contested nature of this understanding. This emphasis will also provide readers with a better understanding of one of the reasons that anthropologists consider issues of **sovereignty** and other forms of political critique, opposition, and dissent that I introduce in this chapter.

Sovereignty, the Body, and the State

A Very Brief History of the Putin Era in Russia

Although Vladimir Putin's governance has many facets, among analysts there seems to exist a tenuous agreement that in 2000, when Putin first came to power, he was intending to be an authoritarian leader, but also one who would allow some small degree of pluralism in politics, and some larger degree of liberalism in private life and business, even if only on the purely pragmatic grounds that he was aware of the limitations of centralized government from Soviet times. But as the years have shown, Putin has found it personally intolerable to be criticized, let along thwarted, so the freedom to oppose him soon disappeared. Elections have become public displays of support for the regime, just like parades, and there appears to be a general agreement that in the Russian Federation Soviet institutional understandings have survived with almost no change. For example, many commentators have noted a marked lack of political transparency in governance, an increase in cronyism and nepotism, and Putin's strong support of the *siloviki*, members of the security services and armed forces. Putin's 2003 arrest of Mikhail Khodorovsky, the head of the oil conglomerate Yukos, marked a watershed moment in the president's increasingly authoritarian regime. While the Russian government argued that the arrest was about Khodorovsky's possible tax evasions, its critics contended that his company posed a threat to government-sponsored oil companies and that Khodorovsky's political ambitions, including his funding of opposition parties (primarily the liberal party *Yabloko*, but also the Communist Party) threatened Putin. In 2015 the Russian politician Boris Nemtsov, who was one of the most prominent and powerful leaders of Russia's political opposition, was assassinated in Moscow near the Kremlin.

Until quite recently, a significant portion of the Russian population associated Putin's presidency with economic stability, recovery, and growth. Especially after the chaotic 1990s the initial years of Putin's regime coincided with a rapidly expanding demand for energy, not only in Western Europe, but also in India and China. Russia's oil, gas, and timber resources provided the Russian government with a source of wealth that was easily turned into political power. In *The Depths of Russia: Oil, Power, and Culture after Socialism* Douglas Rogers (2015), for example, shows how in the 1990s in the Urals region in the city of Perm those with close connections to Perm's oil refineries benefited from *petrobarter*—the exchange of oil for goods and services without references to monetary currency—which, in turn, led to the process of elite-making. As oil was central to Putin-era state-building, new managerial, corporate, and political forms developed, and so did new forms of heritage and civil society-making. Especially as the revenues from Russia's oil boom benefited not only the Putin government and state, but also oil-rich localities and regions, the latter were also empowered to speak up—within limits—against policies and directives associated with Putin's government.

A visible crack in Russians' public support for Putin's presidency appeared in December 2011, when tens of thousands of Russians in Moscow and elsewhere took to the streets, shouting "Putin is a thief" and "Russia without Putin," forcing the Kremlin to confront a level of public discontent that had not existed since the 1990s. Protest against Putin's authoritarianism had been mounting since Russia's parliamentary elections on December 4, which—as both domestic and international observers contended—had been tainted by ballot-stuffing and fraud on behalf of Putin's party, United Russia. But equally crucial to Russians' civic unrest, observers said, had been Putin and then-president Dmitry Medvedev's September 2011 joint announcement that at the time of Russia's March 2012 elections Medvedev would hand the presidency back to Putin, and return to his post as prime minister. Ever since Putin's victory in those elections, in periodic intervals, pent-up anger against a political system of corruption, arbitrary arrests, and intimidation has spilled into Russia's streets. In the lead-up to the 2018 presidential elections, Pussy Riot released a pop video deeply critical of Russia's criminal justice system. And Russian opposition leader Alexei Navalny, who was seen as a genuine threat to Putin's re-election, was barred from the race by the country's central electoral commission.

Understanding the Pussy Riot Trial

As Anya Bernstein (2013b) has shown, one key to understanding the Pussy Riot trial is what social analysts call the sovereign function of the state. Anthropologists have suggested that the state does not represent a reified and unitary entity, but rather an assemblage of practices and techniques that extend into the arenas of sovereignty, body, and gender (Navaro-Yashin 2002; Aretxaga 2003). Building on Max Weber's (1958) contention that one defining feature of the state is its monopoly over violence, anthropologists also call this power political sovereignty, meaning that the state is endowed with the power to decide who should be included as a "good citizen" within its boundaries, and who could or should be punished or excluded. What tends to be important in anthropological analyses of sovereignty is that in its exercise something "rotten"—for example, the abuse of power—is revealed that tends to expose sovereign power as violent, uncivic, and cruel.

Although the law-making function of the state tends to be considered the hallmark of a state's sovereignty, another important site through which the state asserts its sovereignty is the material realm of the body. As Bernstein argues, throughout Russian history bodies, especially female bodies, have been the site on which a number of Russian states exercised their sovereign power. In seventeenth-century Russia, for example, a quintessential instrument of imperial sovereignty was the *knout*, a stiff thong of a rawhide fastened by a bronze ring to braided leather, which attached to a wooden stick. While at the end of the eighteenth century, the wealthier estates were exempted from being whipped by *knouts*, lower-class women were flogged as much as men. Eventually arguments against the use of the *knout* emerged: it was not only the case that women were considered biologically weaker than men, but also that the shame of being naked and lashed in public compromised women's femininity and maternal roles. As women's reproductive capacities were increasingly viewed as significant— also in relation to the buildup and maintenance of the state—practices of corporal punishment were being replaced by the disciplinary practices of the penitentiary system.

Bernstein draws on this context in order to argue that in the Pussy Riot trial a number of different Russian constituencies—including the Russian government as its sovereign power and the *narod* as the embodiment of Russia's "common people"—saw Tolokonnikova, Alyokhina, and Samutsevich as a threat not only to Orthodox religiosity but to the very stability of the Russian state. In supposedly defiling the sanctity of the church and upsetting the order of the state, Pussy Riot came to be defined as an enemy of both the Russian people and the state. Of course, the definition of Pussy Riot as an enemy of the Russian people and the state is a political act that asserts the sovereignty of the law but also of the state that issues such a claim. In confronting Pussy Riot members with all the violence that the Russian state as a political sovereign was able to use, the state not only attested to its own non-identity with its critics but, more importantly, showed its extraordinary ability to symbolize and execute power by maneuvering women's bodies—including determining what, in the last instance, a proper female body is.

Democracy, Civil Society, and Governmentality

As far as entrenched histories go, Russians' concerns with democracy and, relatedly, civil society, started with *perestroika* and *glasnost*. As a word, "democracy" consists of the compound *demos* (the people) and *cracy* (rule), meaning "the rule of the people." As a participatory form of governance, it contrasts with aristocracy, oligarchy, and tyranny, and also with the condition of being colonized or occupied. Yet as Wendy Brown (2012) has argued, from democracy's etymological origin no convincing argument can be made that democracy inherently entails representation, deliberation, participation, free markets, rights, universality, or even equality. Rather, the term carries with it a simple and purely political claim that the people rule themselves. In addition, anthropologists (Nugent 2008) have argued that democracy marks a historically contingent and unfinished principle, meaning that the term does not specify how political rule should be organized or by which political institutions or conditions democracy is best enabled or secured. It is in this sense, then, that democracy involves a continuous struggle for its own articulation.

In relation to Russia, democracy is often described as footloose or hollow: a shell of what democracy is supposed to be. While Russians critical of Putin's regime also describe *demokratiia* in rather crude terms as *dermokratiia* (shitocracy), political analysts tend to draw on theatrical metaphors such as "staged democracy" or "managed democracy" to capture Russia's "weak," "dysfunctional," "poorly consolidated," and even "failed" democracy. Russia's rule of law is tenuous, with the *siloviki* being open to bribery and political influence, and although formally Russia evinces a multiple party system, a competitive party politics barely exists. As Janine Wedel (1998) has pointed out, in post-socialist countries democracy has often appeared as a brand, defined as an entrepreneurial and market-oriented concept from and for the West, and as an (unfulfilled) political promise attached to ideas of political choice, the recognition of cultural and political rights, and citizens' participation. It is also for these reasons that in Russia democracy tends to be regarded as a sham.

In the 1990s in Russia, civil society organizations—non-governmental and informal (*neformaly*) organizations and institutions that tend to manifest the political interests and concerns of a country's citizens—were seen as a crucial sign of the country's democratization. As foreign funding and donor support—for example, by the Ford Foundation, MacArthur Foundation, United States Agency for International Development (USAID), and Carnegie Foundation—flowed into the country, and as their grants became indispensable to the political work of Russian civil society organizations, they also began to determine the agendas of Russian organizations. For example, in her study of the women's group *Zhenskii Svet* (Women's Light) in Tver', a provincial city located 170 kilometers outside Moscow, Julie Hemment (2007) has shown how the social agenda of *Zhenskii Svet* was increasingly dominated by the political perspectives of US or Western European donors. In the 1990s, *Zhenskii Svet* set up a crisis center called *Gortensia* (named in honor of Hortensia, a noblewoman in ancient Rome who spoke out against militarization), including a telephone hotline, individual consultations, and free and legal counseling for victims of domestic violence. Although *Gortensia* was welcomed by women in Tver' and its surrounding communities, one of the center's continuous challenges consisted in bringing across to Western donors Russian women's views that domestic violence is not only a gender issue but also an economic one. In other words, *Gortensia*'s local insights and knowledge that in Russia issues of domestic violence were and are attached to Russians' experience of the transition were dismissed by foreign funding bodies as irrelevant. As a result, Russian civil society organizations were and are uneasily situated **53** between the interests and insights of their constituents and the perspectives of Western financial backers, and they are thus—by necessity—sometimes complicit with Western policies.

Building on the French philosopher Michel Foucault's (1926–84) concept of **governmentality**, Hemment argues that the funding provided by foreign donors is not simply altruistic but, in fact, constitutes a form of governance that influences and shapes the behavior of Russian civil society organizations. Governmentality, for Foucault ([1984] 1991) implied not only the array of institutions, apparatuses, and regulations that manage and shape social life, but also the ways in which these systems influence or guide the conduct of human beings by acting upon their circumstances, desires, and hopes. There are at least three important aspects to Foucault's use of the term *governmentality*. One element is that the term governmentality essentially refers to the *conduct of conduct*: that is, to the more or less calculated ways of thinking and acting that regulate and shape the conduct of individuals or groups toward specific goals. A second element is that the term points to a refusal to reduce political power to the activities of the state. And the third element is that the principal target of government is not politics but people and populations. In other words, governmentality indexes those strategies and tactics that shape human conduct and bodies in particular ways.

Protest and the Public Sphere in Russia

As the Pussy Riot trial and the demonstrations mentioned above show, activists in Russia have started to wage campaigns against the government and the state. As a means of mobilization and a form of communication, the internet has been especially powerful in this regard. For example, during the sizeable protests against President Putin in 2011–13, Facebook, Twitter, and LiveJournal became important platforms for articulating protest and dissent. In seeking to create an effective **public sphere**—meaning a space where citizen-actors can gather to discuss issues of common interest or public concern—activists also sought to open up a space in which political discussions were neither ruled by the state nor by the marketplace but by citizens' agency. Most critical Russian commentators seem to agree that in contemporary Russia the creation of a functioning public sphere has suffered. For example, in 2013 an amendment to the Law on Public Gatherings changed the definition to allow police to classify any group of people as engaging in a "public gathering." Violating the rules on public gatherings—an elastic term to begin with—results in a fine the equivalent of US$1,500, a crippling amount for many Russians. In the sphere of civil society, 2013 also saw the emergence of a law that requires nongovernmental organizations that receive foreign funding to register as "foreign agents": a requirement which subjects them to paralyzing financial reporting standards but also marks them—by implication—as hostile to the Russian government.

In anthropology there exists an extensive literature on the politics of autocratic and corrupt regimes, as well as the ways in which people have sought political agency to contest and resist such regimes. This is a literature that covers a great deal of conceptual ground which I cannot rehash here, but one important strand focuses on the ways in which opposition and dissent are articulated and performed. For example, in an early but groundbreaking discussion James Scott (1990) argued that opposition is not always open and overt but also articulates itself through cultural forms such as popular poetry, jokes, street wisdom, political satire, songs, and the popular memory of the martyrs and heroes of former protests. In making a distinction between "public transcripts," which he describes as open interactions between subordinated people and those who are in power and determine what can be said in public, and "hidden transcripts," by which he means modes of agency and resistance that occur under the shield of masquerade and disguise, Scott also criticizes binary or dualistic conceptualizations of power and resistance to open up investigations for more nuanced explorations of protest, solidarity, social movements, and collaboration.

A Very Brief History of Protest and Social Movements in Russia

Although to contemporary observers it may seem as if a Russian history of protest and dissent began with the 2011–13 anti-Putin protests in Moscow, in fact Russia has known a long record of protest and dissent (Venturi 2001). Historian Richard Stites (1989) has documented the emergence of feminist, anarchist, and social justice-oriented social movements in nineteenth-century Russia, as well as the utopian visions that existed in 1920s revolutionary Russia. However, when Stalin rose to power in the mid-1920s, experimental approaches to both politics and the arts disappeared, especially as they were displaced by a cultural iconography that centered on Stalin's power. As Alexei Yurchak (2006) has shown, in 1950s and 1960s Russia film and music, as well as fashion and style, became important means to express one's distance from the state. One example were the *stilyagi* (from *stil'*—style), a relatively small subculture of Soviet youth influenced by American films shown in Soviet cinemas, as well as other Western cultural-material expressions. Then there were the *tusovski*, a slang term used for non-institutionalized "scenes" of people with some shared interest in "hanging out" and discussing themes that could not be talked about in official ways. Leningrad's café Saigon was one place that in the 1960s and 1970s provided a space for these alternative discussions and interactions. And then there were the "bards" like Bulat Okudzhava and Vladimir Vysotskii, who sang about the dehumanizing aspects of Soviet life. During the Soviet period, many of Vysotskii's songs were not released by the state-run recording label *Melodiia*, but they were distributed by means of illegal tape recordings (*magnitizdat*) and a personal and private distribution system. And, of course, as the brief discussion in Chapter 3 of Douglas Rogers's (2009) work on Old Believers has shown, dissent could also be religious and spiritual in content and form.

While in the mid-1980s the hope for political and cultural change returned with *glasnost* and *perestroika*, as the descriptions in Chapter 2 have illustrated, in the 1990s many Russians had adopted a politically cynical attitude and felt simply worn out. It was thus not before the years 2005 and 2006 that protest would visibly emerge in Russia again. In a series of opposition protests that in those years took place in a number of major Russian cities, including St. Petersburg, Moscow, Ekaterinburg, and Vladivostok, hundreds of thousands of people demonstrated against Putin's program of neoliberalism or monetization (*monetizatsiia*), which had replaced the remaining Soviet social welfare benefits. For several weeks thousands of people blocked roads and administrative buildings, demanding the restoration of welfare benefits, which included free or heavily subsidized medicine and transportation for pensioners and war veterans with set financial allowances. In the same year Russian chess champion Garry Kasparov started to hammer out a small coalition of those who opposed Vladimir Putin, participating in the so-called Marches of the Dissenters. The appellation brought back the importance of the notion of dissent that in the 1960s and 1970s had been made famous by Russian dissidents including Solzhenitsyn, Brodsky, and Sakharov. While these protesters were heroes in the West, for many Russians their practice of exposing the lies underpinning the Soviet political system was considered meaningless because then the very system seemed resistant to change. Other dissonant voices, especially those associated with literature and the arts, withdrew to the countryside.

While in the 1990s, Russians tended to be portrayed as apolitical and apathetic (Mickiewicz 2014), after 2005–06 this assessment began to change. In 2007 and 2008 in Moscow the Khimki Forest Protests, steered by Yevgenia Chirikova, emerged. In demonstrating against the Russian government's plan to build a highway through a birch and oak forest situated at the perimeter of Moscow, protestors held rallies, built encampments, and communicated their concerns about the forest's environmental destruction through blogs on the internet. As many of the demonstrations and rallies were unauthorized, riot police put them down violently. As one consequence, Chirikova sought change from within and ran in Khimki's municipal elections, only to see her election campaign decisively crushed by Putin's party, *United Russia*.

When in December 2011 Vladimir Putin announced his intention to run for Russia's presidency again, large-scale protests broke out in Moscow, growing in intensity on December 24. Demanding freedom for political prisoners, an official investigation into electoral fraud, and new democratic and open elections, protestors carried posters and placards with slogans that expressed their desire for a more substantial democracy and—more concretely—their opposition to vote rigging. Within this context lawyer and anti-corruption blogger Alexei Navalny rose to prominence as one of the most significant voices of the protest movement. In calling *United Russia* a "Party of Crooks and Thieves," he supplied the language for a variety of protestors to talk about many things stolen from them: not only money and government services, but also hopes for democracy and—more concretely—votes. Together with others, Navalny also dug through publicly available information to expose the often absurd amounts the Russian government was spending on the simplest and most necessary things— like the toilets in government buildings—and the real estate and cars that Russian officials owned, but which they would never be able to afford on their actual salaries. In early 2017 in Russian urban centers, after Navalny had publicly aired a film in which he alleged that former Russian prime minister Dmitry Medvedev commanded vast personal wealth through a network of foundations, rallies occurred again.

In the wake of Putin's March 2012 election to his third term as president two massive May protests in Moscow's Bolotnaya Square continued to expose people's dissatisfaction with the regime. Bound in the north by the Moscow River and in the south by a wide canal, Bolotnaya Square is an artificial island that can only be reached by bridges. While in the May 2 demonstration protesters were still free to enter and leave the island as they wished, in the succeeding May 6 demonstrations riot police closed off access to the bridges. As thousands of people were jammed in on the island, violent fights between protesters and riot police broke out, leaving a number of wounded on both sides. Although in the aftermath of these events governmental crackdown continues to be severe, for a number of Russians the mass demonstrations have nevertheless been the grounds for a modest optimism and hope.

Figure 5.1 Moscow, 2013. Preparing for a demonstration.
Photo by the author

Ethnographic Close-Up. On July 12, 2013, in Theater Square in Moscow around 30 Russian activists were arrested. Their crime: on Russia Day, one of the country's national holidays, they had tried to stage a protest on Moscow's Theater Square, adjacent to the city's famous Red Square. Objecting above all to Moscow's increasing gentrification—the process of "upgrading" particular spaces to make them appealing for upscale shopping, living, and hanging out—they stood near the Bolshoi Theater holding small placards with the word *net* (no) either printed or handwritten on them. They were also chanting the word. As it turned out, police clad in riot gear had already been waiting for them. In fact, the demonstration had barely started when the police began to train their clubs on the protesters: arms were twisted, hands were cuffed, and some people were kicked to the ground. Forcefully pushed into police vans, the protesters were then driven to local police stations and detention centers. Almost immediately, activists and friends formed a telephone chain to find out who had been taken where, to support comrades, and to put pressure on the police. Approximately two days later, most of the protesters had been released.

On the night before the protest, I spent time with two activist friends who found themselves in a fierce disagreement over the political logic of the Theater Square *aktion*. The discussion turned on issues related to the protest's strategic organization and effectiveness, and the risks associated with going through with it in the first place. One of my friends, Sergei, had decided against participating in the *aktion*, arguing that it amounted to nothing more than a spectacle and ritual, to a formulaic and standardized performance that would not yield any political change or progressive effects. In contrast Sasha, who had decided to participate in the *aktion*, argued that it was important to publicly show that protest matters, that not everybody—as the government tended to assume—was lethargic and apathetic, that some people were still able to summon the power to care. Although he knew that the protestors would not be victorious and that, in fact, the *aktion* would not shift the ground to allow for a more democratic political system in Russia, it appeared critical to him to stage attempts to disrupt governmental assumptions that protest could always already be suppressed and did not matter. Although the *aktion* would not offer a corrective to Putin's politics or attack the mechanisms of its top-down democracy, it would nevertheless stand as a sign of people's agency and protest.

The discussion between Sasha and Sergei as sketched out above brings to light some of the difficulties of political organizing in Russia. It raises questions about the means by which to organize opposition and protest, but it also raised questions about the protest's purpose and meaning. While the *aktion* emphasizes the desire of at least one part of a Russian critical public to express its dissatisfaction with and opposition to Russia's current regime, it also remains stuck in a ritualistic display of dissent that does not open up new vistas for innovative political tactics and imaginations. It is, indeed, for these reasons that for Sergei the *aktion* represents an empty and pointless ritual. At the same time, though, it makes political power visible, projecting dissent in dramatic ways.

As Mischa Gabowitsch (2017) has shown in his work on the 2011–13 protest movement, metaphors of ritual, spectacle, and performance are certainly very apt when speaking about protest politics in Russia. In arguing that democratic elections themselves mark a ritual—one that in the Russian case was painfully violated by vote rigging—Gabowitsch draws on a long line of social science thinking about the theater-state, a notion made famous in Clifford Geertz's (1980) work on nineteenth-century Bali. In describing the Balinese theater-state as one based on dramaturgical elements of power—the imaginative display of flowers, temples, ornaments, and carvings, and the performative power of dances, melodies, postures, masks, and gestures—Geertz also argues that the theater-state creates a poetics of power that dramatizes it as blessed, stable, and sacred: as a state that is not conducive to change and transition. As Gabowitsch shows, it is then against this sham that protestors continue to struggle. What, under these circumstances, would mark a meaningful politics of opposition? As if to mirror the politics of the theater-state, in the example of the *aktion* that I described above the emphasis is on symbolism. Yet in their efforts to produce more politically effective forms of agency, activists continue to struggle to embrace both symbolic and institutional forms of protest that—in the end—do not only articulate their discontent but also provide real change to the theater-state.

Suggested Discussion Questions

What does it mean to speak of the state, and in particular the Russian state, in terms of sovereignty? What means of agency and dissent do critics of the current Russian state have at their disposal? How effective are these means? What is the relationship between authoritarianism and democracy? Why is Putin's regime appreciated by some Russian citizens and not by others?

Suggestions for Further Reading

Beumers, Birgit, Alexander Etkind, Olga Gurova, et al., eds. 2017. *Cultural Forms of Protest in Russia*. London: Routledge.

Bennetts, Marc. 2014. *Kicking the Kremlin: Russia's New Dissidents and the Battle to Topple Putin*. London: Oneworld.

Das, Veena, and Deborah Poole, eds. 2004. *Anthropology in the Margins of the State*. Santa Fe: School of American Research Press.

Dragadze, Tamara. 1995. "Politics and Anthropology in Russia." *Anthropology Today* 11 (4): 1–3. https://doi.org/10.2307/2783104.

Gessen, Masha. 2014. *Words will Break Cement: The Passion of Pussy Riot*. New York: Riverhead Books.

Hann, Chris, and Elizabeth Dunn, eds. 1996. *Civil Society: Challenging Western Models*. New York: Routledge.

Ortner, Sherry. 1995. "Resistance and the Problem of Ethnographic Refusal." *Comparative Studies in Society and History* 37(1): 173–93. https://doi.org/10.1017/S0010417500019587.

Paley, Julia. 2001. *Marketing Democracy: Power and Social Movements in Post-Dictatorship Chile*. Berkeley: University of California Press.

Sharma, Aradhana, and Akhil Gupta, eds. 2006. *The Anthropology of the State: A Reader*. Malden, MA: Blackwell Publishing.

CHAPTER 6

GENDER, SEX, AND DESIRE

Ethnographic Close-Up

In 2015 I spent March 8 with a number of female and male friends in the northern Kamchatka Peninsula in the small city of Ossora. Around the world March 8 marks International Women's Day: a day that celebrates the social, economic, cultural, and political achievements of women, and that also stands as a call to action for accelerating gender parity. Not affiliated with a particular political party or group, the day brings together a number of institutions and organizations to advocate for women's rights. While International Women's Day has been observed since the early 1900s, following the 1918 Revolution in Russia it was turned into an official holiday. In 1945 in Soviet Russia, on March 8 the country began to specifically acknowledge the tremendous work of women in construction, their heroism in World War II or the Great Patriotic War, and their struggle for peace.

The apartment of my friends in Ossora is small, consisting of a minuscule kitchen and two bedrooms, one of which also serves as a living room. By the late afternoon of March 8, my three female friends had a produced a veritable Russian feast that was served on one of the very low couch tables that stood in the bedroom/living room: *ukha*, a warm fish broth; *pelmeni*, pork meat wrapped in a thin flour dough; *kotlety*, small pan-fried meatballs; *pirozhki*, small pies filled with mashed potatoes and dill, as well as with mushrooms and onions; and a spectacular-looking *sel'd pod shuboy*, chopped salted herring under a blanket of cooked and shredded red beets. A sizeable *pirog*, a baked case of dough filled with sweet raspberry jam, was served as dessert. It had taken my three friends more than six hours to put this feast on the table.

While my female friends had worked without pause in the kitchen to prepare the meal, their boyfriends and husbands had been spending the same hours in the bedroom/living room whiling the time away: smoking, drinking vodka and beer, and playing *durak*, a card game where it is one's goal to rid one's self as soon as possible of all cards. Legs stretched out before them, they also—at times drunk, impatient, and bored—waited. While girlfriends and wives took responsibility for the management of the day and preparation of the feast, I did not see or hear any of the men offering help. Neither, it needs to be said, did I hear any of my friends asking for help.

Gender Trouble in Russia

In the brief snapshot provided above, gender relations appear in a very traditional way, stereotypical almost to a breaking point. Women cook, while men are served. Women dress up, while men play cards, smoke cigarettes, and lounge on couches. And, in the end, women clean. Although it could reasonably be assumed that *glasnost* and democratization in Russia would have also brought more openness in terms of gender relations, analysts (Goscilo 2014; Pilkington 1996; Rethmann 2001) have pointed out that in contemporary Russia gender relations continue to be marked by an emphasis on traditional masculine qualities, including physical strength, aggression, and "being the man of the house." Buoyed by governmental and religious ideologies and institutions, including Vladimir Putin's male posturing—since 2000, Putin has had himself photographed riding horses bare-chested, tracking and shooting tigers (with a tranquilizing dart), shooting a whale with a crossbow to garner a skin sample, piloting a firefighting jet, swimming a Siberian river, steering a Formula One race car, riding with a motorcycle gang, and cheering as part of the crowd at heavyweight fighting events—in contemporary Russia gender relations are marked by a rather traditional focus on weak femininity, strong masculinity, and the general disavowal of queer sexualities. As Valerie Sperling (2015) has argued, contemporary gender politics in Russia are driven by the idea of a **hegemonic masculinity**, by which Sperling means the exclusive conferment of positive values on one exclusive idea of maleness, and the resultant reinforcement of certain characteristics—women are weak, men are strong—in Russia's gender order as a whole. In other words, gender as a concept of identity is tethered to a mythic masculine norm.

Like anywhere else, in Russia the persistence of hegemonic ideals of masculinity—its solidity and stability—is not necessarily assured but must always be shored up against other realities and myths. For example, in contemporary Russia dominant ideals of masculinity are often established in antagonistic relation to supposedly Western ideals of masculinity—with

Western men being associated with "weak" characteristics, such as being neat, clean, romantic, and respectful to women. While this binary logic is rooted in an East (Russia)–West (Western Europe, North America) divide that readers have already encountered elsewhere in this book, it also helps to define the figure of the *muzhik,* meaning a man who is tough, powerful, and strong. While in the early Soviet era a *muzhik* tended to be portrayed as a male peasant—as counter-revolutionary, backward, and ignorant, especially when compared with the revolutionary worker—in the post-Soviet period the term *muzhik* has gained a positive valence. Yet no equivalent movement has taken place for women. For example, as Elizabeth Wood (1997) has shown, in the early Soviet period the female equivalent of *muzhik* was *baba,* a derogatory term for a peasant woman or a woman of limited intellectual scope. In contemporary Russia the latter has certainly maintained its pejorative connotations, and continues to be used as an offensive and deeply insulting term.

At the beginning of the 1990s in Russia a small but vocal feminist movement emerged, which included organizations such as the Moscow Gender Center, St. Petersburg Center for Gender Problems, the Association of Sexual Minorities, and the All-Union Committee of Soldiers' Mothers. In the face of often open hostilities and pressure, feminist and queer analysts in Russia began to offer critical reflections on Russian gender policies, practices, and norms (Kon 1995; Temkina and Rotkirch 1997). These critiques included the recognition that in Russia gender norms are not only based on rather stereotypical ideas about masculinity and femininity, but that they are also used to legitimize forms of male competitiveness, aggression, militarism, and Putin's presidency. In general, men are advantaged over women in terms of securing a job, salary, and being promoted in corporate and government positions. Social commentators (Gessen 2017) have reported that there are high rates of domestic and homophobic violence, that reports of rape are often dismissed or "disappear," and that—in general—misogyny serves as a tool of authority-building. It is within this context that feminist and queer groups fight for the rights of women to leave a violent relationship, for a person's right to choose her, his, or their sexual behavior and partner, and for non-homophobic legislation.

In this chapter I explore the politics of gender identities in Russia. I begin by briefly providing a definitional history of gender to move on to a brief history of gender relations in Russia. In focusing this discussion on issues related to employment and household relations, I do not seek to perpetuate traditional gender stereotypes but rather to build on what Sarah Ashwin (2012) has described as Russia's quintessential gender order, in which men always tend to come out on top. In the second part of the chapter I focus on the relationship between women and issues of reproductive health in Russia. In recent years, anguished debates about the reproductive fate of the nation have raised questions about women's morality and health, as well as about the ways in which cultural notions of gender underpin views on reproduction. In considering the ways in which women feel that they have to work on themselves to make the "right" life choices and decisions, I also draw the analysis into the arena of neoliberalism that I briefly introduced in Chapter 2. In the third section I open up the inquiry of gender in the anthropology of Russia to briefly examine queer activism, with *queer* implying the willful rejection of the hegemony of sexual and gender normativities. Originally used as a term of denigration (and still seen by many as derogatory), in this chapter "queer" signifies a liberatory project whose strength lies in its exploitation of the gaps in conventional categories of identity and expression. Although still associated primarily with "same-sexual-object choice," the personal and political reclaiming of the term queer also signals sexual and gender possibilities that can't be captured by a binary gender framework at all.

What Is Gender?

A critical issue in debates about the significance of gender is the diversely gendered nature of bodies and the tactile nature of diverse bodily practices. The recognition that the body is not the source and locus of identity has been animated by the thought of the French philosopher Michel Foucault ([1984] 1991), whom readers already encountered in Chapter 5, and by Judith Butler (1990), who argues that the body is never a neutral site of cultural significations but a critical site of discipline and regulation. What Foucault and Butler mean by this is that disciplinary modes of power—for example, the ways in which particular institutions render gender categories and identities as stable through the imposition of forms of compulsory heterosexuality—mold and form bodies. In taking issue with essentialist premises of sexuality that link gender identities to the body, and by recognizing that gender is always "made" (Ortner 1996) in culturally, socially, and historically specific ways, they ask under what discursive and institutional conditions biological differences become the salient characteristics of gender. For example, when people ask, "Isn't the capacity to give birth a matter of biological differences?" they are not really asking a question about the materiality of the body. What they are actually asking is whether or not the social institution of reproduction is the most salient one for thinking about gender.

Of course, these connections and categorizations are not just abstract ideas that scholars in feminist, gender, and queer studies think about—as social analysts have shown, they are embodied in the ways in which people see themselves and live their lives. Butler and others employ the concept of **performativity** to describe the ways in which social scripts about sex and gender are enacted. The word "performativity" is closely associated with "performance," and the artifice that we associate with the theater is an important part of it. A key difference between performance and performativity, however, is that "performance" conveys the idea of an actor playing a role. With performativity, however, there is no "real" identity prior to its scripted enactment. In other words, gender identities are not grounded in a stable or absolute truth, but are rather made to seem "natural" through repeated performance. It is through the dynamic of repetition that identities are confirmed, but also—crucially—destabilized, in the sense that performance can once and for all confirm the truth of the ideal—or the myth that it is trying to interpret.

For some people some of the time, gender identity is something that they inhabit so comfortably that they are hardly aware of it; to them, the idea that all of us are engaged in interpretation or performance seems bizarre. But for people whose lived experiences resonate awkwardly with cultural norms, the performative nature of identity is more visible and, as Butler suggests, open to re-signification or subversion. For example, in the 1990s in Russia, Vladik Mamyshev-Monroe, a visual artist, drag queen, and social media icon for gay rights who publicly experimented with gender identities and was not afraid to speak out against homophobia in Russia, began to build on notions of *glamur* (glamour) that had started to develop in the 1990s (Goscilo and Strukov 2011). Especially between 1995 and 2000 Russian editions of magazines owned by global media corporations, including *Cosmopolitan, Elle, Harper's Bazaar, Marie Claire*, and *Vogue*, entered the Russian market, replete with advertisements about makeup, clothes, diet tips, and advice for makeovers and plastic surgery. Whereas before Soviet representations of women had tended to play up the image of a supposedly sexless worker, now women were being asked to add a new and often highly sexualized dimension to their appearance. In a series of performative roles, Mamyshev-Monroe exaggerated symbolic markers of femininity—including makeup and dress—drawing spectacular attention to their artificiality while, at the same time, destabilizing and re-signifying the normative understandings on which these were based.

A Brief History of Gender in Contemporary Russia

There is little question that for the duration of the Soviet Union from the perspective of the state the most important role for women and men was that of the worker. Since the early Soviet period, at the heart of this identity has been the assumption that citizens existed to serve the state and to build socialism, with work representing a quasi-compulsory form of social integration in the Soviet era. In addition, political scientist Gail Lapidus (1978) has also pointed out that work was an economic necessity since Soviet wage scales and pensions were premised on the idea of a dual-earner family. Yet in spite of their apparent radicalism in integrating women into the labor force, the Bolshevik regime continued to emphasize women's roles as mothers, which tended to be understood as a political-demographic duty to the socialist state and not as a private matter. What's more, neither the Bolsheviks nor their successors challenged the idea of domestic work as incontestably feminine. Rather, instead of keeping it in the private sphere, the Bolsheviks sought to bring it out into the public, where women were then paid to perform it. Thus, in spite of a number of significant changes in the realm of gender from previous regimes, in Soviet Russia gender hierarchies were preserved: the acceptance of a supposedly natural sexual difference on the part of the new communist elite informed what was expected of women as mothers and wives, and the terms on which they were integrated into the labor force.

66

For both women and men, the gender order of the Soviet system had a number of significant implications. First, in terms of the distribution of labor, it was deeply unbalanced. In addition to working full-time in the labor force—often for substantially lower pay than men—women were also expected to take primary responsibility for domestic duties. Even as working motherhood was facilitated by nurseries, kindergartens, clubs for schoolchildren, and summer camps, women tended to experience a "dual burden"—meaning that women were expected not only to labor extensively in the work force but also within the context of the family, where they tended to assume full responsibility for household chores and children's care. In spite of all rhetoric to the contrary, this "double burden" was never problematized in the Soviet Union, and given the political monopoly of the Communist Party and comprehensive censorship in this arena, there existed almost no opportunities for women themselves to develop a critique of their situation through organization and debate. Both at home and in the labor market, gender inequality was preserved.

Although in 1991 the collapse of the Soviet Union brought along with it hopes that in the new Russia a more egalitarian gender order would emerge, this did not really happen. In the late 1980s political reformer Mikhail Gorbachev had famously argued that women should return to their "mission" in the home, and vocally worried about the public costs of emancipation. This assessment was widely shared even among the new political élite, and thus in the 1990s new gender policies were not systematically put in place. Instead, the gendered order of the economic transition also meant that the privatization of "the market" appeared in deeply sex-segregated ways, making it tremendously difficult for women to obtain high-paying jobs or even equal pay (Marsch 1996; Buckley 1997; Bridger, Kay, and Pinnick 1996), and that the demise of social(ist) state policies—including the privatization of state-subsidized kindergartens— meant that women's contributions to the household continued to be more important than ever. As men continued to increase their presence in the once female-dominated but now deeply lucrative spheres of banking and commerce, women were increasingly shunted away into the poorly paid arenas of education and health care.

Russian gender norms, of course, do not just have implications for women, but also for men. While at first glance it may seem as if most men enjoy an advantaged position in the economic and social sphere, their reality often takes a different shape. First, in the 1990s the role of primary bread-winner proved to be deeply challenging and this pressure only gradually began to ease in the 2000s. As one consequence, men frequently experienced high levels of anxiety, both regarding their position in established families and their ability to form a family in the first place. Second, men's status as fathers remains fragile. Following a divorce, men have very little chance of gaining custody of their children, even if emotionally and socially they are clearly better positioned to take care of their kids. And third, because alcohol consumption is one important element in Russian images of the *muzhik*, it sometimes appears to be the case that men resort more easily to drink than women. As one consequence, men also tend to experience greater health risks than women.

Gender and Reproduction in Russia

Within the anthropology of Russia and Eastern Europe, gender and issues of reproductive health have been of central importance to anthropologists (Rivkin-Fish 2005; Gal and Kligman 2000). One reason why this is the case is that throughout much of the history of the Soviet Union abortion was a government-sanctioned and widely used means of contraception and means of maintaining reproductive health that—simultaneously—was also officially derided and dismissed. While in 1920 the Soviet Union became the first country to legalize abortion, in 1936 Stalin recriminalized the practice as part of his drive to increase the Soviet Union's birth rate. Even as in 1955 Soviet leader Nikita Khrushchev legalized abortion to make the process safe again, the Soviet government continued to denounce abortion as both immoral and dangerous, and as an antisocial act testifying to women's rejection of motherhood. At the same time, it also made very little effort to improve the conditions for women's reproductive health. In many cases, women endured abortions in large wards without any privacy, and often even without anesthesia. Other contraceptive means such as condoms, diaphragms, vaginal rings, and oral pills were rarely available and when they were, it was certainly not over the counter.

Another reason for the Soviet Union's ambivalence toward abortion is that in the 1980s the annual number of deaths began to exceed the number of births, generating anguished debates about population decline and the fate of the Russian nation. As phrases such as "dying out" (*vymi-ranie*) and extinction were increasingly used in public discourse, Russian politicians started to advocate for the implementation of pro-natalist policies, the withdrawing of funding for family planning, and a ban on abortion. In arguing that the survival of the nation rested on Russian women's abilities and desire to bear children and to raise these children in nuclear families, Russian politicians tended to imagine and construct women's bodies as birthing machines. Paradoxically, in contemporary Russia this functional, instrumental, and—from a liberal perspective—derogatory view has ushered in certain improvements in maternal health: for example, increasing government contributions for childcare and augmenting mothers' pension funds.

In the 1990s Michele Rivkin-Fish (2005) conducted ethnographic research at a maternal health care institution in St. Petersburg. Interested in what kind of changes pregnant and birthing women, as well as Russian health care providers, envisioned and sought for the improvement of women's reproductive health, Rivkin-Fish noticed a fundamental paradox: even as Russian health professionals and non-Russian health organizations were interested in some form of collective and even governmental action to better women's situations, pregnant and birthing women largely seemed to dismiss such routes. For example, Rivkin-Fish reports that women frequently refused to engage with debates that took place at family-planning centers and which focused on reproductive politics and women's health as a social and collective good. Instead, women tended to argue that improvement of reproductive health conditions would come with the transformation of female attitudes, values, and behavior. For example, in arguing that women should abstain from having multiple sexual partners, wearing sexually suggestive and attractive clothing, speaking crudely, drinking, and smoking, many of the women whom Rivkin-Fish knew and with whom she worked expressed the sentiment that it was up to them to produce optimal health outcomes. In other words, a number of women had increasingly come to see reproductive health as a matter of individual control and responsibility, deeply related to their virtue, ethical capacities, and reasoning.

From a liberal Western perspective, it would be easy to dismiss these women's reactions as traditionalist and conservative. At first glance, they certainly fit easily with the piety asked for by Orthodox Church and other gender-conformist institutions. However, by situating women's reactions within the context of the transition that was marked by increasing neo-liberalization and privatization, Rivkin-Fish argues that women's focus on morality is directly related to the ways in which discourses of consumerism and pleasure are infused with moralistic messages about responsibility and female virtue. Thus, instead of necessarily agreeing with progressive health officials' complaints about the diminishing role of the state in managing the health of populations—and also recognizing the fact that the role of the state in Soviet reproductive politics was always problematic to begin with—women began to see forms of moral and physical self-improvement as elements of their reproductive health and, by extension, life. While from a governmental perspective the women that Rivkin-Fish knew had seemingly subjected themselves to a regulatory framework based on personal and bodily discipline, from the perspective of the women themselves, moral behavior and virtuous practices of the body constituted the means through which better health outcomes could be realized.

Similarly, in an extensive work that investigates the politics and experience of single motherhood in Russia, Jennifer Utrata (2015) describes how single mothers in Russia feel that they need to work on themselves—harden and manage their emotions, hold back tears, aspire to treat problems as "temporary unpleasantness," stamp out traces of self-pity, and steel themselves to deal with life—to make up for the systemic failures of the state. In labeling this emotional and cultural work "practical realism," by which Utrata means a presentation of one's self as positive and not—for example— despairing, she analyzes how women do not necessarily hope for better family politics, social welfare conditions, or stable and caring relationships (although they might find all of this desirable), but build on notions of autonomy and self-reliance to support their families and themselves. In other words, women's "practical realism" resonates deeply with Russia's newfound neoliberal ideology that has been marked by—among other things—the economic and social shrinking of the state. In being able to rely on personal family connections and networks, including grandmothers, single mothers are to some extent able to cushion the manifold economic and cultural pressures that come along with single-parenting.

Queering Russia

Shortly before the Winter Olympics took place in Sochi in 2014, homophobic anxieties in Russia found their most salient expression in the passing of new legislation. In June 2013 in a unanimous vote—436 to 0—the Duma passed a law to ban the distribution of "propaganda of non-traditional sexual relationships to minors in Russia." Intentionally rather vaguely framed, in essence the law made it illegal to distribute materials on LGBTQ sexuality and rights, and—by extension—to put homosexual and queer sexuality on an equal footing with heterosexual relations. As article 6.21 of the Code of the Russian Federation on Administrative Offenses was approved and signed by Vladimir Putin, feminist and LGBTQ activists in Moscow, St. Petersburg, Rostov-on-Don, and other cities demonstrated against Russia's legal institutionalization of heterosexual gender norms. In protesting against this law, they also protested against politicians' bigotry and intolerance, sexual harassment and discrimination, and a long and entrenched history of homophobia in Russia that continues into the present. For example, even liberal parties like *Yabloko* (Apple) have not assumed an official stance against sexual discrimination. In other words, the (hetero) sexualization of politics, which—as we have seen above—relies on a clear delineation of masculinity and femininity, also extends into the realm of same-sex and queer love. Legislation and other political legitimation strategies based on homophobia and sexism reinforce sexual discrimination nationwide, and also help to support a rather narrow representation of gender standpoints in political centers. While, from a certain perspective, this form of representation may be considered as undemocratic, it certainly continues to perpetuate the harmful effects of rigid gender norms and understandings.

Although there exist a number of historical indications that in Russia gay and lesbian communities have always existed (Healey 2001; Kelly 1999), such communities have also always exemplified sexual desires that could or should not be mentioned in public ways. While anti-gay and sodomy laws were in place throughout the history of the Soviet Union, as Dan Healey (2014) has argued, it was especially with the end of World War II that homosexuality came to be seen as a form of sexual pollution and contamination. This was largely the case because after 1945 in Russia anxieties over population loss had grown rampant, and the Soviet regime had become eager to establish pro-natalist policies and norms. In addition, a considerable part of the Soviet public had come to see the forced labor camps of the GULAG system as "hothouses" of supposed sexual perversion. Certainly until the late 1980s, the Soviet Union mobilized medicine and law to contain queer sexualities: men who were engaged in or found guilty of participating in homosexual sex frequently became the subjects of psychiatric scrutiny or imprisonment. Women who desired other women were sometimes allowed to fly "under the radar"—precisely because women were seen as more loving, emotional, and physically tender to begin with—but, like queer men, they too were subjected to "medical treatment," that, as it did for men, entailed the prescription of libido-suppressing drugs and compulsory registration as psychiatric outpatients with nasty consequences in everyday life.

To build up networks of solidarity and to help counteract socially discriminatory effects, in the 1970s and 1980s Russia's queer community began to organize itself. Initially meeting in private apartments in *kruzhki*, among small circles of friends that were not always confined to discussions of sexuality, queer activists began to develop a sharpened understanding of Soviet homophobia. By the end of the 1980s these *kruzhki* had developed into an important reference point for the rise of openly gay and lesbian activism. In 1989 Soviet Russia's Association of Sexual Minorities (ASM) supported the appearance of the first Soviet gay and lesbian magazine, entitled *Tema*. Between 1990 and 1991, the ASM hosted several media conferences in Moscow, calling for the decriminalization of homosexuality and governmental recognition of queer sexuality. As many of these conferences were funded by Western organizations, including the European Union and associations in the United States, significant parts of the Russian government and public did not look favorably upon them. In the mid-1990s foreign sponsorship of Russian organizations started to dry out, often causing associations like the ASM to lose their funding. However, cultural productions in the form of newsletters, autobiography, and fiction continued.

Although in the anthropology of Russia ethnographic studies of queer sexuality are still few and far between, a few analyses have emerged. Building on ethnographic fieldwork done in the mid-1980s, Laurie Essig (2012) describes how a queer underground scene (*tusovka*), including music, bars, clubs, newspapers, and literature, existed at urban local levels. Recently Veronika Lapina defended her doctoral research entitled "Queer Nomads: In-Country Mobility of Sexual Becomings in Russia," which—at the time of this writing—she is preparing for publication. Francesca Stella (2013) has examined how the visibility of queer sexualities and identities assisted Moscow to frame itself as the self-consciously cosmopolitan capital of Russia. In showing that queer subjects in Moscow experience more freedom than queer subjects in Russian provincial cities, she argues that the former are increasingly able to occupy public space. At the same time, she shows how the Moscow city administration's banning of the June 2011 gay pride parade—in a burst of homophobic efficiency, in June 2012 a Moscow court banned pride events in the city for the next hundred years—hurt the city's internal reputation. Ever since that year, pride events in Moscow have been illegal, although queer activists continue to organize them on annual basis, only to be shut down by anti-pride protestors and the police.

Suggested Discussion Questions

How are gender relations structured in Russia, and why are they structured this way? What is the significance of reproduction in the context of gender relations? Why do women feel that they have to "work on themselves"? For what purpose? Why is Russia's current regime opposed to queer rights?

Suggestions for Further Reading

Attwood, Lynne. "The Post-Soviet Woman in the Move to the Market: A Return to Domesticity and Dependence?" In *Women in Russia and Ukraine*, edited by Rosalind J. Marsh, 255–66. Cambridge: Cambridge University Press.

Baer, Brian J. 2009. *Other Russias: Homosexuality and the Crisis of Post-Soviet Identity*. New York: Palgrave Macmillan. https://doi.org/10.1057/9780230620384.

Funk, Nanette, and Magda Mueller, eds. 1993. *Gender Politics and Post-Communism: Reflections from Eastern Europe and the Former Soviet Union.* New York: Routledge.

Gessen, Masha. 1994. *The Rights of Lesbians and Gay Men in the Russian Federation.* San Francisco: International Lesbian and Gay Men Human Rights Commission.

Goldman, Wendy Z. 1993. *Women, the State, and Revolution: Soviet Family Policy and Social Life, 1917–1936.* Cambridge: Cambridge University Press. https://doi.org/10.1017/CBO9780511665158.

Goscilo, Helena, and Beth Holmgren, eds. 1996. *Russia. Women. Culture.* Bloomington: Indiana University Press.

Hubbs, Joanna. 1988. *The Feminine Myth in Russian Culture.* Bloomington: Indiana University Press.

Kon, Igor S., and James Riordan, eds. 1993. *Sex and Russian Society.* London: Pluto Press.

Lenskyj, Helen Jefferson. 2014. *Sexual Diversity and the Sochi 2014 Olympics: No More Rainbows.* New York: Palgrave Macmillan. https://doi.org/10.1057/9781137399762.

Pilkington, Hilary, ed. 1996. *Gender, Generation, and Identity in Contemporary Russia.* New York: Routledge. https://doi.org/10.4324/9780203219089.

Rivkin-Fish, Michele. 2010. "Pronatalism, Gender Politics, and the Renewal of Family Support in Russia: Toward a Feminist Anthropology of 'Maternity Capital.'" *Slavic Review* 69 (3): 701–24. https://doi.org/10.1017/S0037677900012201.

Stites, Richard. 1978. *The Women's Liberation Movement in Russia: Feminism, Nihilism, and Bolshevism, 1860–1930.* Princeton: Princeton University Press.

CHAPTER 7

MEDIA AND ART

In the summer of 2013 I participated in a workshop in Moscow's Andrei Sakharov Center, named after the Soviet physicist who in 1975 was awarded the Nobel Prize for Peace only to be exiled in 1980 to the city of Gorky, today's Nizhny Novgorod. The workshop was run by three Russian journalists and political activists who had been trained by Internews, an international nonprofit organization whose mission it is to support independent TV, radio, print, and online media sources to train journalists in ethical and investigative journalism and to assist traditional **media** outlets in creating interactive media presences. The workshop's emphasis centered on the possibilities for Russian journalists to speak out against political censorship and repression. A sober mood pervaded the room. This was not only because in 2007 Internews had been prohibited from operating in Russia any longer (in April of that year Russian police had raided the office of Internews's Russian subsidiary Educated Media Foundation, confiscating computers and arresting then-director Manana Aslamazyan for spurious tax reasons), but also because Russia's relatively broad range of media outlets had failed to produce a more open society. How, participants asked, could they advocate for freer and more open forms of journalism in Russia?

As journalists at the workshop remarked, even as contemporary Russia enjoys a dizzying array of media, news-making tends to be rather difficult and bland. This is not only because the exuberant energy that marked *perestroika*-era news-making could not be sustained in the 1990s, but also because—as Nadezhda Azhgikhina (2008) has suggested—in contemporary Russia the media have become a tool for state communication rather than a vehicle for independent news distribution. Indeed, at the workshop participants expressed deep concerns about state interference in public media, as well as the political and physical violence directed especially against investigative journalists and their writings. Ever since October 2006, when Anna Politkovskaya, a staff writer for Russia's critical newspaper *Novaya Gazeta* who had become known for her fearless reporting on the wars in Chechnya, was shot in a contract killing in her apartment building in Moscow—other violent journalistic deaths include those of Igor Dunnikov, Yuri Shchekochikhin, Paul Khlebnikov, Magomed Yevloyev, and Telman Alishayev—Russian critical journalists have been shaken to their cores. While the Russian government launched a supposedly official investigation into Politkovskaya's death, it quickly faltered, with pro-Russian circles claiming that Chechen warlords had ordered the killing of the journalist, and more liberal and Western-oriented circles asserting that the Putin government had played a central role in her contract killing.

74

The brief exploration above highlights a variety of issues related to media politics in contemporary Russia, including the curtailment of journalistic freedom. Here it serves as the point of departure for a brief discussion of the status of media—print, radio, television, cable and satellite broadcasting, the internet—and media-making in contemporary Russia. I begin by providing a brief historical overview of news-making in Russia. This is a deeply complex story that I can tell here only in a very condensed form. I then move on to a delineation of what anthropologists (Boyer and Yurchak 2010; Roudakova 2017) have identified as Russia's contemporary culture of cynicism to set the stage for understanding one of the attempts by the St. Petersburg–Moscow philosophical and political art collective *chto delat'* (what is to be done?) to think about media in more politically engaged ways. The story that I tell here also could have been integrated into Chapter 5, as it exemplifies one of the many overlaps between media and art in Russia.

In the second part of this chapter I shift gears, away from the arena of media to the realm of **art**: images, objects, designs, dance, literature, songs, poems, and stories. When thinking about art, many readers may envision images such as Ilya Repin's famous 1873 painting *Barge Haulers on the Volga,* Kazimir Malevich's painting *Black Square on a White Background* that in 1915 was exhibited in the *Petrograd 0.10: The Last Futurist Exhibition,* or Vladimir Tatlin's sculpture *Monument to the Third International.* Some readers may also think of museal institutions like the Hermitage, Tretyakov Gallery, Garazh, or Vinzavod, or Russia's National Centres for Contemporary Art (NCAA). Alternatively, they may think about art in terms of particular exhibition practices (Ssorin-Chaikov 2006). In this chapter I situate my investigation of art in the realm of what Lena Jonson (2015) has identified as "dissenting art," which—following her—I take to be art that defines itself in terms of critique and opposition.

I begin the second part's exploration of art with a brief explication of George Faraday's (2000) work on the connection between nationalism and filmmaking. In harking back to the discussion of nationalism provided in Chapter 4, here my focus will be on the ways in which artistic filmmaking in the 1990s mirrored Russia's difficulties while at the same time seeking to remake Russia. I then skip many years to provide a brief history of art as it has emerged around the 2011–13 protests: a point that holds deep significance for many artist groups I mention here. In focusing this chapter's last section on the practices of the art group *voina* (war), I briefly introduce it within the context of discussions about the relationship between art, the **avant-garde**, and democracy. This discussion may feel more abstract than previous ones, but it reflects many conversations that I had, and many comments that I heard, in Russia.

Media

From the perspective of critical analyses of media in anthropology and beyond, it is crucial to recognize that news and information do not offer a transparent window onto the world. Rather, as anthropologists (Boyer 2013) and others have shown, news tends to be assembled from a mass of chaotic data according to particular selection principles, and to be ordered according to particular organizational and political codes. In this sense, the news tends to reflect a limited range of interests—many of which support the preservation of existing power relations—and to rely on "thin" methods of information-gathering. Faced by time and resource pressures, newsmakers such as journalists rely on a steady supply of sources—institutional, governmental, the police, the courts, accredited experts, academics, think tanks, leaders of interest groups—that also set the terms by which news stories are shaped, although news agencies work hard to conceal their partiality or bias.

A Brief History of the Media in Russia

During the Soviet period, as Natalia Roudakova (2017) and Thomas Wolfe (2005) have shown, the media were often portrayed as coercive, dull, and stagnant. As all official media were either owned or controlled by the party, the state, or an official trade organization, and as all news programs originated from the same news agencies—TASS (Telegraph Agency of the Soviet Union) for national news and APN (Agence Press Novosti, now Russian International Agency Novosti) for international news and longer features—in Soviet Russia the media did not greatly differ in the content they presented. However, at the same time the Soviet media landscape was more diverse than has often been assumed (Beumers 2005; Oates 2006). As Yurchak (2006) has shown, there existed a number of underground newspapers and unofficial communication channels that produced communities of *svoi*: communities defined as "our kind of person." Thomas Wolfe (2005) has pointed to the *ocherk*, an essay-like and lyrical genre of writing, as one popular means to discuss controversial stories and themes in the Soviet press. Even as more conventional analyses of Soviet media relations tend to gloss over these aspects, the existence of communicative approaches and means—including *samizdat*, which involved the clandestine copying and distribution of literature banned by the state (Oushakine 2001)—is important for understanding Soviet media relations.

It was against this background that the innovations of *glasnost* stood out. In the mid-1980s in Soviet Russia, print publications like the so-called thick journals (*tolstye zhurnaly*) *Znamia* (Banner), *Oktiabr'* (October), *Nash sovremennik* (Our Contemporary), *Novyi Mir* (New World), *Druzhba narodov* (Friendship of the Peoples), *Ogenek* (Fire) and *Iunost'* (Youth) began to publish political and literary texts that heretofore had been banned, and in the visual sphere television turned into an exciting medium. In stressing the importance of timeliness (*operativnost'*) in news-making—breaking the news as it happened—Gorbachev advocated for the creation of a *telemost*, a space bridge between two news studios in different places. The first space bridge took place in February 1986 between studios in Leningrad and Seattle and was followed in the same year by a bridge between Moscow and Kabul. In October 1987 the First Channel started the program *Vzgliad* (Viewpoint), initially shown on Fridays as a late-evening show. Most presenters of the *Vzgliad* news-making team had been hired from the foreign section of Radio Moscow, since this was the Soviet news section that was most knowledgeable about a Western-style approach to news. As *Vzgliad* began to cover a number of sensitive themes—such as young Afghan students talking about the Soviet invasion in Afghanistan—its journalists became stars. In 1989 Interfax, the Soviet Union's first independent news agency, was formed, and in the same year the Soviet state would end its practice of jamming foreign radio stations. Even as all of these developments were deeply exciting, though, they also exposed the limits of *glasnost*. In 1991 *Vzgliad* had come under attack for its controversial coverage of the war in Afghanistan and the events in Vilnius and, as a result, it was cancelled. Even as the Soviet population had begun to appreciate and recognize the importance of a variety of media outlets and a plurality of opinions, *glasnost* offered no remedies to the country's multiple problems.

With increasing privatization in Russia in the 1990s, media ownership—including both state-owned and commercial media—became convoluted and complex, so much so that it became increasingly difficult to track. In particular the oligarchs, who tended to support media programs that offered critical assessments of Russian politics, began to buy up and run entire media outlets. In 1993 media mogul Vladimir Gusinsky, who also owned the media holding *Most* (Bridge), developed Russia's first state-independent channel, NTV. Quickly gaining fame for its weekly critical political magazines *Itogi* (Sources) and *Segodnia* (Today), NTV added communicational variety to Russia's two state-owned and heretofore solely nationwide channels: the First Channel, which had been established in 1960, and the Second Channel, which had been established in 1982 to largely transmit second-rate material left over from the First Channel. In April 2001, Gazprom, a partially state-owned gas company, assumed control of NTV and removed a number of critical journalists who had run *Itogi* and *Segodnia* from office. The virtual liquidation of independent television deprived millions of Russian citizens of the opportunity to hear a range of news voices, with radio—especially the station *Ekho Moskvy*—tending to be the only source to openly criticize the current regime. In contemporary **77** Russia, satellite television (like national newspapers) remains relatively expensive, and many people simply cannot afford subscriptions. As a result, state-run television stations tend to exert considerable influence. At the same time, the sphere of digital media—cell phones, the internet, emails, the blogosphere, digital radios, webcams, and podcasts—has grown considerably, and has been able to gain some influence of its own. For example, opposition leader Alexei Navalny, who was mentioned in Chapter 5, has made effective use of online campaigning, including YouTube clips, to promote his political anti-corruption platforms. However, it also needs to be said that there is some evidence that the Russian government is starting to control important Russian news aggregators, including Yandex News. For example, in January 2017 a new piece of legislation passed stating that Russian news aggregators have to pay a fine if they publish an item on their front pages that turns out to be incorrect. But if a false piece appears that was written by a registered media outlet (the Russian government controls this registry), then the law will not be enforced. Since it is very difficult or even impossible for an independent online media outlet to obtain such a registration, the law forces news aggregators to exclude media outlets that are not registered with or sponsored by the government.

Cynicism, Putin, and the Media

As a number of anthropological commentators have shown, cynicism has become a dominant sentiment in contemporary Russian culture, including media culture. Cynicism manifests itself in suspicion and open distrust against the powerful, jadedness toward politics and politicians, and weariness concerning revelations of corruption and other forms of "muckraking." As a negative emotion, cynicism is also closely related to de-politicization as the withdrawal from—or absence of—political engagement, including voting. As a particular expression of disenchantment with political life in Russia (and elsewhere), cynicism also tends to prevent the initiation of projects of positive change.

According to Natalia Roudakova (2017), it is important to note that Russia's media culture of cynicism is also articulated and actively propagated by the country's highest political levels. For example, shortly after the Russian submarine the *Kursk* had sunk in the Barents Sea in August 2000, killing all 118 persons on board, Putin was interviewed by Larry King on CNN. Putin, who had not interrupted his vacation in Sochi to attend to the tragedy, had come under severe criticism for his ostentatious display of indifference. When asked by King what had happened, Putin famously said: "It sank." Similarly, he commented that the violent death of Anna Politkovskaya had created more problems for the Kremlin than her Kremlin-critical publications ever did. In response to governmental repressions in the media sphere, and in addition to online forms of protest, in Russia an independent—albeit small—print culture has emerged. This is a culture that embraces zine-making projects and open-access publishing as both a political and an intimate involvement with themes of interest to a Russian critical public. Often featuring hand-drawn images, photography, illustration, and graphic design, the artistic visuality of independent publications tends to be interesting and intense. The same is true for their content. In seeking to reduce filters like publishers, distributors, editors, or bosses, artists and activists engaged in self-publishing often also seek to break out of the circuits of government control and capital. Below I introduce an example.

Ethnographic Close-Up. A few years ago I participated in a workshop in St. Petersburg that revolved around questions of alternative media and culture (Rethmann 2016). The workshop had been organized by *chto delat'*, the artistic–political collective that has produced newspapers on a regular basis since its beginning in 2001. Published usually in English and Russian, with some issues only appearing in Russian, each edition numbers between one and two sheets (between four and eight pages), is hand-printed in editions of 200 to 1,000, and appears in approximately A3 size, with covers that are not uniform, except for the number and date printed on each issue. Members of *chto delat'* tend to distribute these newspapers at events for free.

Each issue of the newspaper reflects *chto-delat*'s interests. The collective has published newspapers on "love and politics," "states of emergency," "the question of revolution and resistance," "the experience of *perestroika*," "the use of art," and an issue on the suppression of critical journalism in Russia bearing the name of the Zapatista slogan "basta" (enough is enough), the revolutionary aesthetics of Bertolt Brecht, and the possibilities for a new and progressive politics. Later issues have covered the themes of the city, artistic struggle, industries of knowledge, the notion of the commons, and film. In considering the possibilities for a progressive and transformative politics for today, each edition aims to circumvent Russian media politics in order to trace the relationship between news-making, political possibility, and cultural production. While the newspaper obviously represents the collective's own

Figure 7.1 Cover page of one of *chto delat*'s newspapers.

Photo by the author, graphics by Natalya Pershina (Gluklya)

interests, its existence also seeks to call into question the parameters of a supposedly apolitical and journalistic landscape through writing about issues and themes with which Russian newspapers will not engage.

From the perspective of *chto delat'*, the news-making project is important because it is not attached to media corporations, media trademarks, or brand names, and addresses readers not as individual consumers but as citizens of an engaged public. In discussions with members of the collective it also became clear that *chto delat'* sees the newspaper as an important political intervention, one that seeks to directly address the cynicism that—as outlined above—tends to pervade Russian culture. Here news-making appears not as a distrustful or derisive exercise, as a form of incorrect or even "fake news," but as an open, authentic, and sincere project (Yurchak 2008b): a project that is driven by a serious desire for social change and the creation of a political landscape in which news is presented in a more truthful way.

Art

Historically, art and anthropology have had a complicated relationship. One of the reasons for this is that anthropology and art are based on different forms of judgment. However, as Alexei Yurchak (2008a; 2008b) has shown, in the anthropology of Russia these fields tend to be more aligned than in other arenas of anthropology because in Russia art has always been an important site to challenge the political status quo. What's more, artistic techniques closely associated with the history of the Russian avant-garde, such as the principle of montage—a joining together of different elements in a variety of combinations based on cinematic editing as developed by Russian directors Eisenstein and Dziga Vertov—has had wide-reaching implications for anthropology (Suhr and Willerslev 2013). For example, in an ethnography otherwise unrelated to the anthropology of Russia, the anthropologist Michael Taussig (1986) put to use the montage-inspired principles of juxtaposition and fragmentation to disrupt a tradition of monological and straightforward ethnographic storytelling.

The Work of Media and the Reclamation of Russia

The anthropologist George Faraday decided to conclude his book *Revolt of the Filmmakers: The Struggle for Artistic Autonomy and the Fall of the Soviet Film Industry* (2000) with an in-depth look at the Russian film *Burnt by the Sun* (*Utomlonnye solntsem*). Directed in 1994 by Nikita Mikhalkov, one of contemporary Russia's most famous filmmakers, the film takes place in the mid-1930s, in the time of the purges and of Stalin's intensifying "cult of personality." It tells the story of the ostensible destruction of Red Army commander Sergei Kotov's family in the summer of 1936, including his supposed demise in the Great Terror, the death of his wife in the GULAG, and the suicide of his romantic and—to some extent—political nemesis Mitia, who works for the Soviet political police or NKVD. When *Burnt by the Sun* won the Academy Award for Best Foreign Language Film in February 1994, Mikhalkov became a star in Russia and on the international scene.

Although the film can be understood on a number of levels, Faraday has shown that it is deeply traditionalist and patriarchal in its political orientation. In presenting certain archaic ways of being, such as a leisured pastoral enchantment with prerevolutionary country estates, *priroda* (nature), *narod* (folk or people), *rodit'* (to give birth), and *rodnoi* (relative; relatedness), the film builds on the Russian notion of *rod*, meaning family or genus. In featuring brass beds, warped gramophones, pitchers with washbasins, lace curtains and old-fashioned guitars, ratty wicker furniture and peasants in traditional linen shirts and dresses, the film also speaks to 1990s Russian concerns over the loss of traditional values in a society that was becoming increasingly consumer-oriented and materialistic. At the same time, the film also constituted a critique of the new artistic individualism and entrepreneurialism that had begun to underlie Russian economic and social life.

Apart from the above-mentioned reasons, why did Faraday pay so much attention to Mikhalkov? As Faraday describes it, in the period of the Soviet Union film as a visual medium had always been popular, but from the early 1960s to the early 1980s alone, the Soviet film industry had managed to maintain a consistent production rate of 120 to 150 films on an annual basis. With an average film attendance of 40 million viewers by the early 1980s—director Vladmir Men'shov's 1980 melodrama *Moscow Doesn't Believe in Tears* (*Moskva slezam ne verit*) alone was seen by 80 million viewers in the first year—the Soviet film industry was doing well. Yet the increasing availability of late-1980s and early-1990s *chernukha* films that showed a degraded domestic and urban existence—as well as the ease with which one could buy pirated versions of Hollywood movies in Russian markets—brought Russian film attendance to its knees. What was needed in the 1990s was a bit of *glamur*: an aesthetic glamour and elegance that would remind Russian audiences of their country's former grandeur. The richly appointed interiors of Mikhalkov's film conjure up memories and interpretations of a supposedly better, because pre-revolutionary, past.

As analysts Helena Goscilo and Vald Strukov (2011) have shown, director Nikita Mikhalkov was not the only one who used the style of *glamur* to entice Russians to forget the *bespredel* and sense of crisis (Chapter 2) that marked the 1990s or Yeltsin years. As in post-Soviet Russia, *glamur* became associated with the stability and prosperity that so many Russians desired; it moved beyond its association with sex-related topics and excessive consumption into the arena of politics and nation-making. For example, artists associated with collective *chto delat'* and others I know regard the restoration of St. Petersburg's opulent Konstantin Palace as a politically

81

associative link to Russia's imperial past, as well as an expression of nationalist and patriotic feelings. Perhaps most ostentatious in this regard is the replica of the Crown of Monomakh (*Shapka Monomakha*)—an ancient and ceremonial jewel-encrusted and sable-lined gold crown that had been used at the coronation of Russian tsars, including Peter the Great—that in 2002 had been reproduced by sixty jewelers to be given to Putin as a gift on his fiftieth birthday. Implying greatness and transcendence, Goscilo and Strukov have argued that in Russia *glamur* has assumed the status of national and quasi-religious salvation.

An Extremely Brief History of Art and Protest in Russia since 2011

It seems fair to say that especially at the end of the first decade of this century Russia experienced a renewed surge of interest in art as a meaningful form of protest.

Frequently inspired by the history of the Russian avant-garde (a disparate artistic movement that used art to think radically about and invent new worlds), **sots-art** (an artistic style that emerged in the 1970s in Russia as a reaction against the official aesthetic doctrines of the state) and *stiob* (a late-Soviet mode of parody that imitated and inhabited the formal features of authoritative discourse to such an extent that it was often difficult to tell whether it was a form of sincere support, subtle ridicule, or a peculiar mixture of the two) emerged as important aesthetic means to reveal the authoritarian discourses propagated by the church and the state. In other words, artists drew not on lavish artistic materials but on humor, parody, laughter, and wit to introduce political ruptures into Russia's governmental fabric. For example, in 2010 protestors in Moscow belonging to the group "Blue Buckets" exhibited a carnivalesque style when they pulled blue buckets over their heads to caricature the *migalki*—a common term for drivers of cars with spinning blue lights on them that allow them to drive at high speed through traffic. The flashing blue lights are often acquired through bribes, and the fantastically reckless driving that goes along with them leads to constant accidents. Protestors thus turned Moscow's main avenues into sites of opposition, slowly walking with blue buckets on their heads across streets, as if to signal that the drivers should get out of their way. At some point the movement was so successful that one demonstration saw dozens of drivers attach blue buckets to their cars in imitation of the official lights. They were also driving at extremely low speed through Moscow.

Another example was the Novosibirsk group *Sinie nosy* (Blue noses) that used the visual means of photography, photomontage, and video installation to expose governmental corruption, hypocrisy, and abuse of power. One of its most famous images featured two policemen kissing in a stereotypical Russian birch forest in the snow. Building on British graffiti artist Banksy's 2004 image "Kissing Bobbies," *sinie nosy* thematized and exposed homosexual desires in Russia, including the ways in which those desires exist in state-related organizations and institutions where the suppression and punishment of such feelings is supposedly at its strongest.

While parody and laughter play a significant role in contemporary Russian artistic culture, performatively and visually more direct forms also have their place. A most obvious example are the dissident practices and art of Pussy Riot that I introduced in Chapter 5. Another example of visually dissenting art was the St. Petersburg Protez group that, at some point, exhibited ten large paintings depicting forms of sexual and domestic violence that exist in Russia today. For her part, the visual artist Victoria Lomasko (2017) has sought through her drawings to recapture the frightful atmosphere that existed in the courtroom during the Pussy Riot trial. Perhaps most radically and shockingly, the performance artist Petr Pavlenskii sewed his mouth shut in political protest against the incarceration of three members of Pussy Riot.

Art and Nonconformity

Ethnographic Close-Up. On the night of June 14, 2010, members and friends of the St. Petersburg-based Russian artistic collective *voina* painted a 65-meter high and 27-meter wide penis on St. Petersburg's Liteiny drawbridge. *Voina*'s activists painted the image, which they titled *chlen* (literally: member; Russian vernacular for penis), in less than 30 seconds, pouring white paint from cans onto the bridge's roadway. The bridge itself is directly located opposite Russia's Federal Security Services (FSB; *Federal'naia Sluzhba Bezopastnasti*—perhaps better known as Russia's successor of the Soviet KGB) building. When, at one o'clock in the morning, the bridge began to open, it shoved not the proverbial finger but rather a dick into the face of the FSB. Predictably enough, the *aktion* provoked a scandal in Russia. On the one hand, it visibly demonstrated a lack of respect toward Russia's government and, by extension, a political statement in the public realm. On the other hand, it raised questions about the definition of political and/or activist art, including the issue of whether *voina*'s action should be considered to be art at all. While members of *voina* were immediately persecuted by the FSB, significant parts of Russia's art scene expressed their support for the group. In April 2011, *voina* won Russia's prestigious Innovation Prize, largely because Russia's art community felt that they needed to show solidarity with the activities of the group.

Formed in February 2007, *voina* initially consisted of a core of philosophy and art students intent on using art to open up and enliven Russia's public sphere. In one of its first performances, *voina* worked with Dmitri Prigov, a Russian dissident poet and sculptor who initiated one of the first performance art pieces by handing out poetic texts to passers-by. The group had been planning an event with Prigov, entitled *Ascension*, which would consist of *voina* members carrying the poet, who would be sitting in an enclosed oak wardrobe, up 22 flights of stairs to the tip of Moscow State University's main building. The *aktion* never happened because Prigov unexpectedly died of a heart attack. To honor the poet and his willingness to work with them, *voina* performed a piece known as *The Wake* or *The Feast*. Instead of ascending to the top of Moscow State University's main building, *voina* descended into the Moscow Metro. Close to midnight they boarded the metro's circle line and quickly set up red plastic tables, which fit perfectly between the benches that run along each side of the subway car. They covered the tables with white tablecloths, and rapidly distributed place settings, bottles of wine and vodka, and traditional Russian bitter and sweet wake fare, all the while reciting Prigov's poems. Even in the eyes of many of *voina*'s detractors, it was a perfect tribute to Prigov. The group videotaped the *aktion*, as it would do with all of its other *aktions* in the future.

After *The Wake*, *voina* launched a series of cumulative *aktions* in which the group commented on Russian politics and life. In February 2008, five couples had sex in Moscow's Biology Museum. The *aktion* was called *Fuck for the Heir Puppy Bear*, a play on Dmitry Medvedev's last name, which derives from the Russian word for bear (*medved*), and who shortly before the *aktion* had been chosen as Putin's successor, essentially to keep the chair warm for Putin for four years. The location for the *aktion* had been chosen for its "natural" associations, including the fact that Putin had recently launched a program to raise Russia's birth rate. Another famous *aktion* took place on November 7, 2008, with the date marking the anniversary of Russia's October revolution. This one was called the *Storming of the White House*. Here members of *voina* had managed to smuggle a powerful laser projector onto the roof of Moscow's Hotel Ukraina, and beamed an enormous skull-and-crossbones image onto Russia's White House, which is situated nearby. It was a spectacular and widely distributed image, but it also raised questions about who was supporting the group, especially since it seemed clear that the laser cannon must have been expensive and difficult to get ahold of.

Voina, or the art of *voina*, has not been easy to like (although the group was never interested in being liked). In fact, it has been condemned from many sides of the Russian public: by the left, who feel that *voina*'s art is too elitist and that the group is too isolated and offers no solution to Russia's problem; by liberals, who feel the same way, but also take issue with the legal shadow status of *voina*'s art; and by ordinary citizens, who feel that *voina*'s art is palpably offensive, self-involved, disdainful of national unity, and contemptuous of public taste. Although *voina* has never publicly responded to its many detractors, it seems clear that it sees its artistic task as to perplex, perhaps repulse, and shock. As a clear adversary of convention, *voina* celebrated the artistic and political margins: not simply by advocating an overturning of conventional aesthetics but by celebrating art as a politically cutting-edge or avant-garde project.

In popular understanding, "avant-garde" has come to mean art that is ahead of its time—shocking, insurrectionary, perhaps even capable of summoning the future. While the term originally emerged from a military context—meaning the front line—in revolutionary Russia it was frequently used to refer to political radicals: Bolsheviks, other socialists, and anarchists. By the mid-twentieth century, the term began to be associated with those artists whose work resonated with the goals of the Russian Revolution: Rodchenko, Tatlin, Mayakovsky, Stepanova, Popova. These artists were reacting to the rigidly conservative art that was then sponsored by national academies. They claimed authenticity only for artworks that challenged familiar and conventional tastes, promoting art that was embattled and battling with the present in the name of the future.

How—with a brief nod to Chapter 4—does a critical, and perhaps even unorthodox, voice in Russia speak out? What makes it possible—given the discussion above—for these voices to enter the public arena? While large democracies like Russia (and elsewhere) rely on mass communication to guide political decision-making, even as they persistently debate the extent to which these means of communication really reflect the will of "the people," as a self-identified part of the avant-garde *voina* sets itself up as a critical voice, questioning both the values of Russia's supposed majority and their expression. *Voina* refuses social pressures to conform or to become a passive consumer of Russia's sham democratic culture. Thus, although *voina*'s art may be called strange, difficult, or elitist, for many people I know it holds a special—even if sometimes begrudgingly so—place in discussions of artist-activists for a more democratic Russia. At the same, *voina* also produced its own mythical status, for its core values were identical with dissent itself.

Suggested Discussion Questions

What is the role of the media in contemporary Russia? What does the suppression of a broad range of free media mean for Russia? What possibilities exist to contest the Russian state's media politics? And what is the role of art in contemporary Russia? Can art be an effective medium in which to challenge Russian politics and policies?

Suggestions for Further Reading

Bernstein, Anya. 2014. "Caution, Religion! Iconoclasm, Secularism, and Ways of Seeing in Post-Soviet Arts Wars." *Public Culture* 26 (3): 419–48. https://doi.org/10.1215/08992363-2683621.

Beumers, Birgit, Stephen Hutchings, and Natalia Rulyova, eds. 2008. *The Post-Soviet Russian Media: Conflicting Signals.* New York: Routledge.

Bishop, Claire. 2012. *Artificial Hells: Participatory Art and the Politics of Spectatorship.* London: Verso.

Buck-Morss, Susan. 2000. *Dreamworld and Catastrophe: The Passing of Mass Utopia in East and West.* Cambridge, MA: MIT Press.

Campbell, Craig. 2014. *Agitating Images: Photography against History in Indigenous Siberia.* Minneapolis: University of Minnesota Press. https://doi.org/10.5749/minnesota/9780816681051.001.0001.

Cushman, Thomas. 1995. *Notes from Underground: Rock Music Counterculture in Russia.* Albany: State University of New York Press.

Hutchings, Stephen, and Natalia Rulyova. 2009. *Television and Culture in Putin's Russia: Remote Control.* London: Routledge.

Mickiewicz, Ellen. 2008. *Changing Channels: Television, Power, and the Public in Russia.* Durham: Duke University Press. https://doi.org/10.1017/CBO9780511491016.

Oates, Sarah. 2013. *Revolution Stalled: The Political Limits of the Internet in the Post-Soviet Sphere.* Oxford: Oxford University Press. https://doi.org/10.1093/acprof:oso/9780199735952.001.0001.

Peters, Benjamin. 2016. *How Not to Network a Nation: The Uneasy History of the Soviet Internet.* Cambridge, Mass.: MIT Press. https://doi.org/10.7551/mitpress/9780262034180.001.0001.

Stites, Richard. 1989. *Revolutionary Dreams: Utopian Vision and Experimental Life in the Russian Revolution.* Oxford: Oxford University Press.

CHAPTER 8

RUSSIA BEYOND RUSSIA

Throughout this book, and especially in Chapter 4, I've talked about Russia as a site of identity, nationalism, and belonging. In that chapter, the focus was on the bounded and geopolitical context of the Russian Federation, although I also mentioned in Chapter 2 how in the eras of *perestroika* and "the transition" desires for global consumer products began to emerge. But, as anthropologists and others have pointed out, in the wake of the demise of the Soviet Union not only objects but people, too, began to move. In 1992 in northern Kamchatka I gained a firsthand ethnographic impression of the urgency with which former Soviet citizens discussed questions of **migration** when Ukrainian families, who at that time lived at the Peninsula's northeastern coast, were preparing to return to the newly independent Ukraine. In conversations over tea in homes and in fishing camps, the women and men I knew told me that their preparations were not primarily driven by a desire to leave the Peninsula, but rather by an anxiety over their futures as non-Russian citizens in the Russian Federation. Many people I knew did not trust the new citizenship law that had been introduced in February 1992, which granted Russian citizenship to all those who already resided in the Russian Federation, and to all citizens of the former Soviet Union who had moved to Russia and applied for citizenship before the year 2000. Things, then, simply seemed too unstable.

As commentators (Pilkington 1998; Markowitz 1993; Roberman 2015) have shown, at the beginning of the 1990s in the Russian Federation migration was unpredictable, chaotic, disordered, and messy. Although people had always moved in the era of the Soviet Union—for example, many Ukrainian women and men I knew in Kamchatka had participated in a

1960s labor program that promised good wages, apartments, holidays, and even cars to Soviet citizens who were prepared to live and work in the Soviet Union's far-flung peripheries—movement itself had been restricted by the internal passport (*propiska*) system. When, in the early 1990s, millions of Soviet citizens found themselves living in places that they did not consider "home," migration increased to unprecedented levels. Out of an estimated population of 25 million ethnic Russians living outside of the borders of the newly formed Russian Federation—most notably in Ukraine, Kazakhstan, Estonia, Latvia, and Lithuania—between 1991 and 2000 approximately 3 million Russians returned to the Russian Federation. At the same time, in search of better jobs, skills, and lives, millions of Russians and other post-Soviet citizens migrated out of the bounds of the former Soviet Union, most notably to North America, Israel, and Western Europe.

By "migration" anthropologists (Reed-Danahay and Brettell 2008) mean the mobility and circulation of people, objects, and ideas across local, regional, and national borders. In the anthropology of Russia, migration is an expansive term, including imperial expansion, colonization, industrial transportation, and urbanization, as well as movement within Russia and across Russia's borders. In this chapter I look at forms of migration that carry people beyond the borders of the Russian Federation. This is not to say that I consider the in-migration of, for example, low-skilled and undocumented labor migrants from Tajikistan, Kyrgyzstan, Uzbekistan, and Kazakhstan, or Chechnya, Armenia, and Georgia, unimportant. As Madeleine Reeves (2013) has shown, the wantonness of their living conditions, which involve securing identity documents, finding jobs through social networks, and accepting work and wages that native-born citizens would be reluctant to agree to, and—as Michele Rivkin-Fish and Elena Trubina (2010) have shown—their always already immediate association with drug smuggling, criminality, and violence—are serious issues. Yet as anthropologists of migration argue, these challenges matter as much for migrants outside of Russia as within Russia. In the first part of this chapter I consider the links between transnational mobility and emotionally and sexually intimate relations that are conventionally sidelined in accounts of migration.

In the second part of the chapter I turn my attention to the study of **transnationalism**. Basically, transnationalism indexes the movement of people, corporations, and ideas across borders. In anthropology, it has been used to transcend the discipline's traditional focus on nation-states and nations, to give voice to people and subjects who do not fit neatly into the framework of "nation," and to differentiate the flow of cultural and ideational ties between nations from the ever-growing flow of capital that tends to be more associated with the concept of globalization. In the example that I discuss transnationalism emerges most palpably in the form of what political analysts Margaret Keck and Kathryn Sikkink (1998) have called "transnational advocacy networks," or TANs: voluntary and non-governmental organizations (NGOs) that assist in promoting certain values—depending on their political perspective, anything from civil society research and human rights to a particular brand of Russian conservatism (Kotkina 2017; Engström 2014). In the second part of the chapter, then, the analytical emphasis is on the affective and ideational work that TANs perform.

I end this section with a discussion of the concept of **diaspora**. As a term, "diaspora" describes the dispersal or scattering of a people, by choice or by force, from their homeland to diverse geographical regions. In the wake of the Soviet Union, Russian diaspora communities have emerged in urban centers as far-flung as London, New York, Vancouver, Berlin, and Shanghai. Central to understanding these diasporas has been and is the experience of trans-border migration, as well as the affective ties that bind diaspora communities to their respective homes and homelands. In what follows, I look at some of the reasons that in the 2017 German federal election a significant number of Russian Germans voted for the right-wing party Alternative for Germany (*Alternative für Deutschland*; AfD), and build on the trope of *home* to understand, at least in part, the economic and cultural logic that may have motivated the vote. One issue that should become transparent in this discussion is the fact that homeland and home are not unambiguously straightforward notions.

I would also like to draw attention to a key aspect of the third section's methodology. When discussing the politics of right-wing populist communities, and especially when situating themselves in critical relation to the views that these groups espouse, analysts tend to run up against what cultural sociologist Arlie Hochschild (2016) has called "empathy walls." An empathy wall is an obstacle to a deep understanding of another person, one that can make us feel hostile to those who hold different beliefs and values than we do. Especially in periods of political tumult, many—Russians and non-Russians alike—grasp for quick certainties. More than simply constituting a trope, then, in the third section of this chapter *home* is also a device that assists me in scaling an empathy wall, a vehicle that allows me to understand Germany's AfD vote as more than a straightforward expression of hate. Issues of history, economics, and political culture all need to inform these analyses, and it is far from my intention to engage in a politics of facile scapegoating and blame.

Migration

It would have been justified to include Alexia Bloch's (2017) research on post-Soviet women labor migrants in this book's chapter on gender as much as in this one. In looking at post-Soviet female small-scale shuttle traders (*chelnoki*) who move back and forth between Russian and Turkish centers, including Moscow and Istanbul, Bloch is especially interested in the ways in which transnational migration has marked the emotional worlds of these traders. For example, when considering shame as an initial emotion experienced by a number of women traders, she situates this emotion within a complex context of changing forms of work, empowerment, and the emotional structure of their relationships in Russia and other parts of the post-Soviet Union. She tells the story of Olga, a woman trader who became so successful that she was able to build up her own family business not far from Moscow, and then elucidates the ways in which Olga's migrant labor assisted her to experience pride in her entrepreneurial activities, while also requiring her to downplay her success with her husband. Even as migrant Russian women entrepreneurs show great business acumen, they feel they need to restrain their skills and accomplishments in order to "keep the peace" in the domestic and private sphere.

One key site for transnational migration from the former Soviet Union has been Turkey, where post-Soviet women are in demand for domestic work, small-scale trade, and in the garment and entertainment industries. Within this context, especially post-Soviet women who plan for or end up with long-term stays in Turkey often experience both the desire and necessity to form intimate ties with Turkish men. In negotiating forms of intimacy, post-Soviet women define love as both romantic and strategic, as it will allow them to secure, for example, citizenship through marriage. Being a "kept woman" was another status that post-Soviet women might desire, because it provided them with some measure of economic security and an alternative to unemployment or low-paid employment.

Transnationalism and Belonging

As mentioned above, the concept of transnationalism serves many purposes: assisting anthropologists in overcoming an analytical focus on nations, giving voice to people who do not fit readily into the framework of the nation, and getting a handle on affective attachments that transcend the boundaries of one nation. In early spring 2014 in the eastern Ukrainian Donetsk region transnationalism as an affective and ideational form of belonging sprang to the fore when ethnic Russians who lived in the Ukraine proclaimed the "Independent People's Republic" in Donetsk, and thousands of Russian-identified refugees from the trans-border Donbass region migrated to Russia. As anthropologists (Wanner 1998; Uehling 2004) have pointed out, as a political entity contemporary Ukraine is marked by multiple cultural fragmentations that link its different nationalities to a number of competing perspectives. For example, Ukrainian citizens who live in the western part of Ukraine tend to more easily embrace liberal ideas associated with the European Union and the West, while citizens living in the East tend to look toward the "Russian world" (***russkii mir***) and **Eurasianism** as a significant source of belonging.

In Russian political and transnational discourse, Eurasianism constitutes a dynamic idea with many shadings. In essence, it describes the fact that Russia straddles the boundaries between Europe and Asia (for a more expansive view see Hann [2016]), occupying a dual or middle position between them. In emphasizing Russia's middle or bi-continental position, Eurasianists tend to agree that it is Russia's particular historical, geographical, and political position that marks it as a unique civilization—as one that should exercise a significant historical and political role among many nations. One central aspect of the Eurasian idea is the evaluation of Russian territory. Rather than orienting Russia toward ideas such as individual liberty and economic and political freedom, Eurasianists argue that Russia is closer to Asia than to the West, and should therefore seek inspiration from concepts based on collectivist ideas. Extending beyond the context of the Russian Federation—and in particular relation to Russia's 2014 annexation of Crimea—Eurasianism also marks the return of a number of post-Soviet sites into Russia's ideational fold. The concept is widely discussed in influential Russian right-wing circles, as well as in Turkish and West European right-wing groups (Shekhovtsov 2018).

As Borysenko, Brammer, and Eichhorn (2017) have shown, in the 2014 Ukraine crisis Eurasianism-inspired endeavors "to return" Russians who lived outside the boundaries of the Russian Federation to Russia were facilitated by the *Evraziiskii soiuz molodezhi* (Eurasian Youth Movement), a border-crossing and transnational action network that enjoys strong support in the Donetsk region. Established in 2005 in Moscow, the Eurasian Youth Movement is founded on the idea of Eurasianism, especially as it is propagated by Aleksandr Dugin, who considers liberal ideas to be harmful to Russia and Europe as a victim of these ideas—decadent, ailing, and salvageable only in the context of "freedom fights" from and for Russia. One of the goals of the Eurasian Youth Movement is to promote the welfare, support the activities and institutions, assert the rights, and protect the interests of their ethnonational kin. Such claims are usually made when the ethnonational kin is seen as being threatened by nationalized policies and practices.

Since its foundation, the Eurasian Youth Movement has facilitated transnational forms of belonging in the Eastern Ukraine through particular practices: workshop and conference organizing, or— similar to the *nashi* example that I discussed in Chapter 4—summer camp organizing. Although Borysenko, Brammer, and Eichhorn do not discuss this in detail, the Eurasian Youth Movement also provides a dense network of communication and other meeting channels which connect leaders and other regional actors through digital, ideational, and cultural ties. Apart from emphases on Russian military aggression and might and the analyses of ideological themes, it would thus also be pertinent to examine the digital means that both uphold and delimit transnational ideas and movements.

Diaspora

In the 2017 German federal elections it appears as if a significant segment of Germany's Russian German community voted for Germany's right-wing party Alternative for Germany (*Alternative für Deutschland*; AfD), which eased with 13 per cent into the German parliament (*Bundestag*). In a televised talk show that followed on the heels of the election, AfD party whip Jörg Meuthen asserted that about 50 per cent of the AfD's vote came from Germany's Russian German community. Although I have not been able to confirm this number, according to many press reports it seems that the Russian German vote for the AfD was indeed fairly high. The AfD conducted an intense electoral campaign in areas populated by a high percentage of Russian German immigrants, such as Berlin-Marzahn or Pforzheim-Haidach. The latter electoral district was able two elect two Russian Germans as AfD representatives to the German parliament.

In German politics, the high voter turnout for the AfD has been seen as one expression of the "citizen of rage" (*Wutbürger*), a media-coined term that indexes German citizens who in the wake of Europe's so-called refugee crisis in 2015—in which Germany experienced an influx of approximately 1.1 million refugees from war-torn Syria and Afghanistan—began vehemently and sometimes violently to protest against the "new immigrants." The country's AfD vote is also seen as a sign of critique of German chancellor Angela Merkel's *Willkommenskultur* (welcome culture), a term that indicates Germany's willingness to open its doors to the arriving refugees. In the name of *Willkommenskultur*, throughout the republic, scanty yet efficient refugee camps were established, refugees were put up in private homes, and—although the bureaucracy was chaotic—language education and welfare were provided.

Overall, it needs to be said, that Germany's affirmation of the country's "open-door policy" began to change when on New Year's Eve in Cologne, on the square between the city's world-famous cathedral and train station—approximately 600 German women were sexually assaulted and harassed by several hundred men that many women described as "Arab-looking," "dark-skinned," and "dark-haired" men. In the following days the city's name metamorphosed into a cipher for Islamist violence and—by extension—the supposed endangerment of the German democratic polity through "Islamization," while throughout the rest of Germany cities began to close their swimming pools to immigrants and refugees. Germany's right-wing populist movement Pegida (Patriotic Europeans against the Islamization of the West) began to intensify its so-called Monday Marches in German cities, and then AfD party leaders Frauke Petry and Beatrix von Storch called for shooting orders to keep Syrian refuges out of the country. Markus Soeder, the Bavarian minister for finance, regional development, and home affairs asked for an upper limit for the intake of refugees, and evoked a German *Leitkultur* (leading culture) to protect Germany's "culture of welcome." In general, German feelings of resentment and hatred in relation to Syrian refugees and other North African migrants increased, and the wins of the AfD in the 2017 elections are seen as one consequence of this hate.

Ethnographic Close-Up   On September 27, 2017, three days after Germany's federal election, I received an email message from Mrs. C., a 58-year-old Russian German woman who in 1990 had migrated from Karaganda in Kazakhstan to Dülmen in North Rhine-Westphalia, Germany. In her message, Mrs. C. informed me that after a period of indecision and deliberation she, too, had decided to give her vote to the AfD. The "too" in Mrs. C.'s letter referred to her husband, children, and Russian German relatives and friends who, like her, had also voted for the AfD. In her letter Mrs. C. let me know that she felt that in Germany the AfD currently happened to be the only political party that took the concerns of the German Russian community seriously. In particular she felt that she and her family were no longer able to feel at home in the German Federal Republic.

Of particular significance to Mrs. C.'s feelings was what in Germany has become known as "case Lisa." On January 11, 2016, Lisa F., a 13-year-old Russian German girl with dual citizenship, disappeared from her home in Berlin-Marzahn. Her parents reported her as missing to the police. On the next day Lisa returned home and told her parents that she had been kidnapped by three unknown men of either southern or Arab origin who did not speak German very well. Questioned by the police, she also indicated that she had been beaten and raped by these men. Upon further questioning, Lisa changed her story, saying that she had voluntarily gone along with "these men." Russia's foreign minister Sergei Lavrov began to accuse the German government of concealing Lisa's rape because Germany wanted to be seen as "politically correct." Furthermore, he offered to Lisa and her parents, who continued to support Lisa's first version of the story, the Russian government's assistance should they choose to return to Russia. In response, Germany's foreign minister Frank-Walter Steinmeier rejected Lavrov's allegations and warned Russia to "politicize the case."

The story of Lisa F. was extensively covered in both Russian and German media, with a number of Russian media—significant parts of Germany's

Russian German community tend to watch Russia's Channel I, to which they have access through satellites and the internet—reporting that Lisa F. had been mistreated and held as a "sex slave." Many Russian Germans reacted with anger. On January 24 a considerable crowd of Russian Germans demonstrated in front of the Chancellery in Berlin, holding placards that read: "Our children are in danger," "Protect our women and children," and "We will no longer be silent." On January 29, a spokesperson for the German prosecution told the press that on the night in question Lisa F. had been together with a 19-year-old male friend. As it turned out, Lisa had been experiencing problems at school and at home, and she had not wanted to return to her parents. On that very day, the Russian and German governments decided not to pursue the case any further, and on January 31 a German spokesperson declared that Lisa had admitted that the rape never happened. Nevertheless, in the aftermath of all of this Lisa F.'s mother continued to repeat the allegations made by her daughter.

The reasons that significant parts of Russia's Russian Germany community voted for the AfD are complex, and include social fears and economic disappointments that they experienced in the German Federal Republic. Taking my cue from Mrs. C.'s message to me, here I elucidate some of these disappointments and fears through the metaphor of home. "Home," of course, is a complex term, carrying with its connotations of interiority, origin, native-ness, and safety. The analysis I suggest below is exploratory, building on what cultural analyst Raymond Williams (1977) has called "structures of feeling," by which he means that feelings do not only mark private experiences but also tell social stories. In other words, emotions and feelings form social grooves through which to trace some of the ways in which Russian Germans feel about and experience "home."

A Very Brief History of Russian Germans

Following on the heels of late-1980s diplomatic negotiations between Soviet president Mikhail Gorbachev and German chancellor Helmut Kohl, it is estimated that between 1989 and 1996 approximately 1.5 million Russian German immigrants, mostly from Kazakhstan, arrived in the German Federal Republic. The term "Russian German" is complex, describing an identity that stretches over five distinct political entities: the German empire, the Russian empire, the Soviet Union, the Republic of Kazakhstan, and the contemporary German Federal Republic. Most specifically it emerged in the late eighteenth century when Empress Catherine the Great (1729–96) invited German farmers and craftspeople from rural areas in Germany's south to "settle" agriculturally highly fertile areas along the Black Sea coast and in the southern Volga region. As German peasants were migrating to Imperial Russia, they also began to identify themselves as benevolent colonialists.

In the narratives of Mrs. C. and Lisa F.—as in the narratives of other Russian Germans I know—the Volga German Autonomous Socialist Republic tends to emerge as a continuous and important reference. As I mentioned in Chapter 4, the Soviet Union developed its own unique approach to nation-building. Instead of ruling, as most modern governments have done, by dividing territory into viable economic units for efficient administration, Soviet reformers created tiny islands of self-rule based on their own conceptions of ethnicity. In 1923, the All-Union Central Executive Committee created the Volga German Autonomous Soviet Socialist Republic along the Volga between Saratov and Kamyshin— providing Russian Germans with a quasi-autonomous status. Between 1923 and 1942—and also, it needs to be said, before that period—Russian Germans developed their own educational institutions, villages, and towns. Historical narratives produced by Russian Germans describe how communities enjoyed their own churches, schools, kindergartens, bookstores, and study centers where people could study agronomy, politics, and economics if they aspired to higher administrative positions in Russian centers.

Following the Nazi German invasion on June 22, 1941, Stalin's government began to consider Soviet citizens with a Russian German background as collaborators and deported the entire population to the east, especially to the Urals, Siberia, and Kazakhstan. It is at this point that the narratives of Russian Germans begin to focus on the intense poverty and misery of living they encountered on Kazakhstan's steppes: living in earthen houses, with hundreds of families settling on land which could sustain no more than a dozen households. Politically marginalized, Russian Germans also lived with epithets forged within a context of violence and anti-Soviet aggression, including "fascist" and Nazi.

During *perestroika*, many Russian Germans hoped for their rehabilitation and, if not necessarily for the recreation of the Volga German Autonomous Socialist Republic, then certainly their repatriation to their former villages. Such a move, however, was resisted by both Gorbachev and Yeltsin. It was also resisted by large parts of the Russian population that now lived in the former Volga German Autonomous Socialist Republic, and who themselves feared being displaced. It was on the heels of German unification in 1989 that, through diplomatic negotiations with Gorbachev, then-German chancellor Helmut Kohl negotiated the *Heimkehr* (return to one's home) of the Soviet Union's Russian German community to Germany.

Home as a Structure of Feeling

Home as Myth
As Mrs. C. tells it, when she still lived in Kazakhstan she was excited about her family's life in Germany. This was largely for two reasons. First, as I have

explained in Chapter 2, by the early 1990s living conditions in Russia were marked by the terms *razrukha* or *bespredel*, describing a chaotic mode of living in which most economic, social, and cultural certainties had already begun to disappear. In other conversations Mrs. C. told me that the family had decided to leave their home in Kazakhstan in the hope of greater security: better houses, work, and better pay for work—no more waiting for salaries, no more looking at empty shelves in shops. Germany would be the home where they would be well cared for and, what's more, well regarded. Although she and other Russian Germans she was acquainted with in Kazakhstan knew little about the country to which they were migrating, they sold everything and left.

Although in Germany all Russian Germans were immediately awarded German citizenship, the high hopes of many for the significant betterment of their material circumstances were frequently thwarted. The majority of Russian German migrants arrived in Germany not only in the wake of the dissolution of the Soviet Union, but also on the heels of German reunification. While initially the 1989 unification of West and East Germany was euphorically celebrated, by 1991 this euphoria had faded. While East Germans had begun to remark on their status as Germany's "second-class" citizens, West Germans had begun to complain about the high costs of reunification, including the so-called solidarity tax and the fact that a considerable amount of public funds went into the build-up of East German infrastructure in the form of building reparations and the fixing of roads. In both East and West Germany resentment of migrants began to mount.

Home/Myth as Disappointment

Although many Russian Germans, like Mrs. C., are thankful to the German government, and especially to Chancellor Helmut Kohl, who negotiated the possibility of their migration from Soviet to German territories, once they arrived in Germany, they did not feel especially welcome. In reference to Germany's 2015 "culture of welcome," Mrs. C. said that one source of pain was the fact that in 1992, when she arrived, nobody opened their home to her or her family—unlike, say, in 2015, when Germans willingly opened their homes and wallets for refugees, collected clothes and food, ran errands, and took care of children while refugee migrants talked to and clarified administrative affairs with government officials. Instead, when Mrs. C. arrived in Germany, social democratic politicians like then-party leader Oskar Lafontaine rallied against Russian German migrants because they saw them as labor competition for German workers. (In 2015 Oskar Lafontaine also rallied against Syrian refugees).

A second source of pain for Mrs. C. and other Russian Germans I spoke to has been the fact that many Germans whom they came to know were not only unaware of Russian German social or cultural history, but—even worse—did not seem to care. In fact, Germans born in the Federal Republic did not recognize Russian Germans as "Germans" but continued to consider them "Russians." This was especially the case because many Russian German migrants spoke either no German at all, or—if they did speak some of the language—they spoke with an accent or archaic vocabulary that some Germans judged "strange."

A third source of pain was that in the former Soviet Union many Russian Germans had not been trained in vocational professions but worked as farmers. Once in Germany, numerous Russian Germans experienced a hard time finding work in Germany's service- and technology-oriented economy. As one consequence, many Russian Germans began to rely on the state for their subsistence, receiving remittances through government-sponsored third-sector vocational training or mandatory welfare-for-work programs. Unemployment rates for Russian Germans in areas that I mentioned before (Berlin-Marzahn, Pforzheim-Haidach) remain high.

Home as Political Attachment
In the early 1990s, when many Russian Germans arrived, Germany seemed to be a country secure in the hands of Helmut Kohl as Germany's conservative chancellor. But in 2017, this was no longer the case. In 2005 Angela Merkel had advanced to the position of chancellor, governing together with the more left-wing Social Democratic Party of Germany in coalition. In Mrs. C.'s opinion, under the leadership of Angela Merkel the Christian Democratic Union (CDU) had moved too far to the left, deciding, for instance, to increase the country's minimum wage and to end the use of nuclear energy in Germany. She also struggled with the CDU's abolition of the military draft, with what she considered Germany's far-too-lenient punishment for criminals, as well as the country's endorsement of same-sex unions.

Like other Russian Germans I know, Mrs. C. describes herself as "conservative." Conservatism is a highly complex and value-laden term, but in conversations with Mrs. C. it often emerged in contradistinction to Germany's supposedly liberal culture. For example, take the notion of the "culture of welcome" (*Willkommenskultur*). As a Russian German, Mrs. C. says that she has nothing against the country's Turkish immigrants. But in 2015 *Willkommenskultur* had started to reshuffle the social and cultural order of the country. Both metaphorically and literally, members of Germany's Russian German community had stood in line for work, honor, and the opportunity to be recognized and heard. Somehow, in ways that Mrs. C. resented but could not understand, Syrian refugees had allegedly managed to skip ahead in those lines. In a supposed hierarchy of suffering, their contemporary suffering seemed to matter more than the historical suffering and the social injustices that had happened to Russian Germans—even though, as Mrs. C. indicated, they were Christians and Germans, instead of Muslims and Arabs.

What's more, Mrs. C. felt that Germany's "culture of welcome" was stifling her own right to expression. Both the term and Angela Merkel, she implied, were imposing liberal ideas about who was worthy of sympathy. Mrs. C. did not want to be told whom she should feel sorry for, including Syrian refugees. She and the Russian German community with whom she identified had suffered from war and persecution as well. Again, in Germany nobody had seemed to care. Now Angela Merkel was clearly overstepping her role as the supposed guardian of the county by suggesting to people how to feel and telling them whom to help. And in refusing Germany's "culture of welcome," Mrs. C. did not want to be told that she was a "citizen of rage," a hateful and uncaring person. Like other members of Germany's Russian German community, she preferred to watch the news on Russia's Channel I over YouTube or on satellite television—media platforms that lifted her focus away from the refugees' needs and from her own detachment to them, toward her own and Russian German community needs. Perhaps, then, it was Russia and not Germany that was her ultimate home?

Suggested Discussion Questions

Why and how have issues of migration become significant in the anthropology of Russia? What is the relation between migration and transnationalism, and migration and belonging? How do cultural and political attachments shape belonging and understandings of home, and how do these understandings influence the migrants' experience of living in places that they do not consider home?

Suggestions for Further Reading

Bassin, Mark, Sergey Glebov, and Marlene Laruelle, eds. 2015. *Between Europe and Asia: The Origins, Theories, and Legacies of Russian Eurasianism*. Pittsburgh: University of Pittsburgh Press. https://doi.org/10.2307/j.ctt15nmjch.

Laruelle, Marlene. 2014. *Russia's Arctic Strategies and the Future of the Far North*. New York: M.E. Sharpe.

—, ed. 2015. *Eurasianism and the European Far Right: Reshaping the Europe-Russia Relationship*. Lanham: Lexington Books.

Marcus, George. 1995. "Ethnography in/of the World System: The Emergence of Multi-Sited Ethnography." *Annual Review of Anthropology* 24 (1): 95–117. https://doi.org/10.1146/annurev.an.24.100195.000523.

Nikolko, Milana V., and David Carment, eds. 2017. *Post-Soviet Migration and Diasporas: From Global Perspectives to Everyday Practices*. New York: Palgrave Macmillan, 2017. https://doi.org/10.1007/978-3-319-47773-2.

Pilkington, Hilary, Elena Omel'chenko, Moya Flynn, et al. 2002. *Looking West?: Cultural Globalization and Russian Youth Cultures*. University Park: Pennsylvania State University Press.

Randolph, John, and Eugene M. Avrutin, eds. 2012. *Russia in Motion: Cultures of Human Mobility since 1850*. Urbana: University of Illinois Press.

Scheffel, David. 1991. *In the Shadow of Anti-Christ: The Old Believers of Alberta*. Toronto: University of Toronto Press.

Siegelbaum, Lewis H., and Leslie P. Moch. 2014. *Broad is My Native Land: Repertoires and Regimes of Migration in Russia's Twentieth Century*. Ithaca, NY: Cornell University Press.

99

GLOSSARY

agency the capacity of individuals and collectives to act in independent
and critical ways

art modes of thinking, reflection, and representation by way of images,
objects, designs, dance, literature, songs, poems, and stories

avant-garde new and innovative ideas, especially in the arts, or the
people introducing them

blat' informal exchange and barter system

civil society an aggregate of associations and organizations that operate
independent of the government

Cold War the name for a set of events that made up the international
order between the end of World War II in 1945 and the fall of the
Berlin Wall in 1989

collective memory points to the fact that memory is not just a private
act but also matters in social and cultural ways

commodities services and objects produced for exchange or consumption by someone other than their producers

conspicuous consumption consumption that is obvious, noticeable,
and visible in order to signal class differences and distinctions

constructivism usually defined in opposition to essentialism: the
emphasis is on the historical, cultural, and political circumstances in
which identities are produced

cosmology the organizing logic of particular forms of meaning, such as
religion, nationalism, and culture

culture a concept that is difficult to define, but that tends to include
knowledge, beliefs, art, morals, history, social relations, economics,
customs, sexuality, gender, nationalism, and social relations

democracy consisting of the compounds *demos* (the people) and *cracy*
(rule), the term translates as "the rule of the people." As a participatory form of governance, it contrasts with aristocracy, oligarchy, and
tyranny, and also with the condition of being colonized or occupied.

diaspora describes the dispersal or scattering of a people, by choice or by force, from their homeland to diverse geographical regions

dissidents individuals who challenge an established doctrine, policy, or institution

emic an anthropological approach that seeks to understand people's actions from their own point of view

Enlightenment a perspective that sees history in terms of continual development and progress

essentialism the reduction of a way of being or culture to unchanging and supposedly ahistorical traits

ethnography a theoretically informed description of a particular way of life

Eurasianism a complex idea based on romantic philosophies of empire developed in the 1920s by Russian émigrés, the theory of ethnogenesis as developed by Lev Gumilev, and the right-wing ideas of Aleksandr Dugin. As a movement, Eurasianism is based on the fact that Russia straddles the boundary between Europe and Asia, a geo-political positioning that defines the country as a supposedly unique civilization

fieldwork anthropology's quintessential method; usually a form of long-term residency in a particular community

gender the historical, cultural, and social construction of bodies; gender is not the naturalized difference between women and men, or biologically determined. Rather, gender is "made" in a reiterative process that includes dress codes, behavior, language, and style

glasnost the Russian word for "transparency"; here it refers to a policy that emerged in Soviet Russia in the mid-1980s

globalization social, political, cultural, economic, and technological processes that, taken together, have created the conditions of our interconnected present

governmentality a form of governance that does not simply mean the array of institutions and regulations that manage our life, but also the ways in which these regulations and institutions influence our behavior or conduct

hegemonic masculinity the idea that masculinity and "maleness" means being always already robust, tough, and strong

intelligentsia a status and a class of educated people

identity the way in which we understand ourselves and others

ideology the ideas and ideals that form the basis of economic, political, social, and cultural life

life story a methodological device and mode of representation that offers anthropologists a way of understanding how broader social forces articulate themselves in the life of a person

loss the social experience of disintegration and demise

meaning a term that indexes the purpose or significance of social beliefs and actions

means of production land, tools, factories, technological devices, machinery, and equipment; physical inputs for the production of economic value

media means, tools, and outlets of communication used to deliver information

migration the processes by and ways in which people, ideas, images, messages, technologies, finance, knowledge, and goods travel across borders

nation a complex concept that describes ways of national belonging

nationalism a mode of identification in which political claims are made in the name of the nation

neoliberalism refers to free market economic policies, the privatization of public services, and the dismantling of the welfare state

nostalgia a compound of two words—*nostos* (the return home) and *algos* (grief, pain, sorrow)—that describes feelings of absence and loss

oligarchs extremely wealthy businessmen who gained much of their affluence in the wake of the dissolution of the Soviet Union

participant observation an anthropological method; a form of immersion in the world of others

perestroika the Russian word for "restructuring"; here it refers to a policy that emerged in Soviet Russia in the mid-1980s

performativity indicates that cultural and social meaning is not a given but always "made up" and enacted

public sphere a space where citizen-actors gather to discuss issues of common interest or public concern

post-socialism term that emerged after the demise of the Soviet Union to explain the cultural, political, historical, and economic legacies of socialism

religion the holy, sacred, and revered, and its study

russkii mir extends Russian nationalism into the sphere of geopolitical imaginations, including the national spheres of non-Russian peoples *samizdat* the clandestine copying and distribution of literature banned by the Soviet state

socialism a political and economic theory of social organization that argues that the means of production should be owned or regulated by a community as a whole

sots-art an artistic style that emerged in the 1970s in Russia as a reaction against the official aesthetic doctrines of the state

Soviet Union also Union of Soviet Socialist Republics; a socialist one-party state in Eurasia that existed from 1922–91

sovereignty a term with a number of connotations; here it refers to the law-making function of the state

Stalinism a set of policies, behaviors, and ideas related to Joseph Stalin, including rapid industrialization, collectivization, and the cult of personality

state a nation or territory considered as a political community organized under one government

stiob a late Soviet mode of parody that imitated and inhabited the formal features of Soviet authoritative discourse to such an extent that it was often difficult to tell whether it was a form of sincere support, subtle ridicule, or a peculiar mixture of the two

totalitarianism tends to describe a political system in which all aspects of public and private life are regulated, and in which political power is concentrated in the hands of a few or one leader(s)

transition Russia's move toward democratic governance and a free market economy in the 1990s

transnationalism closely related to migration; the term is also used to transcend analytical foci on the nation-state, and to give voice to people and subjects who do not fit neatly into the framework of nation

West a complex term that marks not necessarily a natural but an imaginary place. Russia and "the West" are often posited in a binary framework, with "the West" either marking a morally debauched or more "European" and democratic place.

REFERENCES

Anderson, Benedict. (1983) 1991. *Imagined Communities: Reflections on the Origin and*   **105**
Spread of Nationalism. Revised and extended edition. New York: Verso.

Anderson, David. 2000. *Identity and Ecology in Arctic Siberia: The Number One Reindeer Brigade.* Oxford: Oxford University Press.

Anderson, David, and Dmitry V. Arzyutov. 2016. "The Construction of Soviet Ethnography and the Peoples of Siberia." *History and Anthropology* 27 (2): 183–209. https://doi.org/10.1080/02757206.2016.1140159.

Appadurai, Arjun, ed. 1986. *The Social Life of Things: Commodities in Cultural Perspective.* Cambridge: Cambridge University Press. https://doi.org/10.1017/CBO9780511819582.

Aretxaga, Begona. 2003. "Maddening States." *Annual Review of Anthropology* 32 (1): 393–410. https://doi.org/10.1146/annurev.anthro.32.061002.093341.

Ashwin, Sarah. 2012. "Gender." In *Routledge Handbook of Russian Politics and Society,* edited by Graeme Gill and James Young, 329–40. New York: Routledge. https://doi.org/10.4324/9780203804490.ch27.

Azhgikhina, Nadezhda. 2008. "The Struggle for Press Freedom in Russia: Reflections of a Russian Journalist." *Europe-Asia Studies* 59 (8): 1245–62.

Baiburin, Albert, Catriona Kelly, and Nikolai Vakhtin, eds. 2012. *Russian Cultural Anthropology after the Collapse of Communism.* New York: Routledge.

Bakhtin, Mikhail M. 1981. *The Dialogic Imagination: Four Essays,* translated by Michael Holquist. Austin: University of Texas Press.

Balzer, Marjorie M. 1999. *The Tenacity of Ethnicity: A Siberian Saga in Global Perspective.* Princeton: Princeton University Press.

—, ed. 1995. *Culture Incarnate: Native Anthropology from Russia.* New York: M.E. Sharpe.

Barker, Adele M., ed. 1999. *Consuming Russia: Popular Culture, Sex, and Society Since Gorbachev.* Durham: Duke University Press.

Bassin, Mark. 2017. "What is More Important: Blood or Soil? *Rasologiia* Contra Eurasianism." In *The Politics of Eurasianism: Identity, Popular Culture, and Russia's Foreign Policy,* edited by Mark Bassin and Gonzalo Pozo, 39–58. London: Rowman & Littlefield.

Bernstein, Anya. 2013a. *Religious Bodies Politic: Rituals of Sovereignty in Buryat Buddhism.* Chicago: University of Chicago Press. https://doi.org/10.7208/chicago/9780226072692.001.0001.

—. 2013b. "An Inadvertent Sacrifice: Body Politics and Sovereign Power in the Pussy Riot Affair." *Critical Inquiry* 40 (1): 220–41. https://doi.org/10.1086/673233.

Beumers, Birgit. 2005. *Pop Culture Russia!: Media, Arts, and Lifestyle.* Santa Barbara: ABC Clio.

Bloch, Alexia. 2017. *Sex, Love, and Migration: Postsocialism, Modernity, and Intimacy from Istanbul to the Arctic.* Ithaca, NY: Cornell University Press.

Bogoraz [Bogoras], Vladimir [Waldemar]. 1904. *The Chukchee: The Jesup North Pacific Expedition 7, Memoirs of the American Museum of Natural History.* New York: G.E. Stewart.

Borysenko, Veronika, Mascha Brammer, and Jonas Eichhorn. 2017. "The Transnational 'Neo-Eurasian' Network and its Preparation of Separatism in Ukraine 2005–2014." In *Transnational Ukraine?: Networks and Ties that Influence(d) Contemporary Ukraine*, edited by Timm Beichelt and Susann Worschech, 225–50. Stuttgart: ibidem-Verlag.

Boyer, Dominic. 2010. "From Algos to Autonomous: Nostalgic Eastern Europe as Postimperial Mania." In *Postcommunist Nostalgia*, edited by Maria Todorova and Zsuzsa Gille, 17–28. New York: Berghahn.

—. 2013. *The Life Informatic: Newsmaking in the Digital Era.* Ithaca, NY: Cornell University Press. https://doi.org/10.7591/cornell/9780801451881.001.0001.

Boyer, Dominic, and Alexei Yurchak. 2010. "American Stiob: Or, What Late-Socialist Aesthetics of Parody Reveal about Contemporary Political Culture in the West." *Cultural Anthropology* 25 (2): 179–221. https://doi.org/10.1111/j.1548-1360.2010.01056.x.

Bridger, Sue, Rebecca Kay, and Kathryn Pinnick. 1996. *No More Heroines? Russia, Women, and the Market.* New York: Routledge.

Brown, Kate. 2004. *Biography of No Place: From Ethnic Borderland to Soviet Heartland.* Princeton: Princeton University Press.

—. 2015. *Dispatches from Utopia: Histories of Places Not Yet Forgotten.* Chicago: University of Chicago Press. https://doi.org/10.7208/chicago/9780226242828.001.0001.

Brown, Wendy. 2012. "We Are All Democrats Now." In *Democracy in What State?*, edited by Giorgio Agamben, 44–57. New York: Columbia University Press.

Brubaker, Rogers. 1996. *Nationalism Reframed: Nationhood and the National Question in the New Europe.* Cambridge: Cambridge University Press. https://doi.org/10.1017/CBO9780511558764.

Buckley, Mary, ed. 1997. *Post-Soviet Women: From the Baltic to Central Asia.* Cambridge: Cambridge University Press. https://doi.org/10.1017/CBO9780511585197.

Butler, Judith. 1990. *Gender Trouble: Feminism and the Subversion of Identity.* New York: Routledge.

Caldwell, Melissa. 2010. *Dacha Idylls: Living Organically in Russia's Countryside.* Berkeley: University of California Press. https://doi.org/10.1525/california/9780520262843.001.0001.

Cervinkova, Hana. 2012. "Postcolonialism, Postsocialism, and the Anthropology of East-Central Europe." *Journal of Postcolonial Writing* 48 (2): 155–63. https://doi.org/10.1080/17449855.2012.658246.

Collier, Stephen. 2011. *Post-Soviet Social: Neoliberalism, Social Modernity, Biopolitics.* Princeton: Princeton University Press. https://doi.org/10.1515/9781400840427.

Essig, Laurie. 2012. *Queer in Russia: A Story about Sex, Self, and the Other*. Durham: Duke University Press. https://doi.org/10.1215/9780822379522.

Etkind, Alexander. 2013. *Warped Mourning: Stories of the Undead in the Land of the Unburied*. Stanford: Stanford University Press.

Faraday, George. 2000. *Revolt of the Filmmakers: The Struggle for Artistic Autonomy and the Fall of the Soviet Film Industry*. University Park: The Pennsylvania State University Press.

Foucault, Michel. (1984) 1991. *History of Sexuality*, Vol. 1, translated by Robert Hurley. Harmondsworth, UK: Penguin.

Gabowitsch, Misha. 2017. *Protest in Putin's Russia*. Cambridge: Polity Press.

Gal, Susan, and Gail Kligman. 2000. *The Politics of Gender after Socialism*. Princeton: Princeton University Press. https://doi.org/10.1515/9781400843008.

Geertz, Clifford. 1980. *Negara: The Theatre State in Nineteenth-Century Bali*. Princeton: Princeton University Press.

Gellner, Ernest. 1990. *Nations and Nationalism*. Oxford: Blackwell.

Gessen, Masha. 2017. *The Future of History: How Totalitarianism Reclaimed Russia*. New York: Riverhead Books.

Goscilo, Helena, ed. 2014. *Putin as Celebrity and Icon*. New York: Routledge.

Goscilo, Helena, and Vlad Strukov. 2011. "Introduction." In *Celebrity and Glamour in Contemporary Russia: Shocking Chic*, edited by Helen Goscilo and Vlad Strukov, 1–26. London: Routledge.

Grant, Bruce. 1995. *In the Soviet House of Culture: A Century of Perestroikas*. Princeton: Princeton University Press.

—. 2001. "New Moscow Monuments, or, States of Innocence." *American Ethnologist* 28 (2): 332–62. https://doi.org/10.1525/ae.2001.28.2.332.

—. 2009. *The Captive and the Gift: Cultural Histories of Sovereignty in Russia and the Caucasus*. Ithaca, NY: Cornell University Press.

Gray, Patty A. 2005. *The Predicament of Chukotka's Indigenous Movement: Post-Soviet Activism in the Russian Far North*. Cambridge: Cambridge University Press.

—. 2016. "Memory, Body, and the Online Researcher: Following Russian Street Demonstrations via Social Media." *American Ethnologist* 43 (3): 500–10. https://doi.org/10.1111/amet.12342.

Gray, Patty A., Nikolai Vakhtin, and Peter Schweitzer. 2003. "Who Owns Siberian Ethnography? A Critical Assessment of a Re-internationalized Field." *Sibirica* 3 (2): 194–216. https://doi.org/10.1080/1361736042000245312.

Halbwachs, Maurice. 1992. *On Collective Memory*, translated by Lewis A. Coser. Chicago: University of Chicago Press.

Hann, Chris. 2016. "A Concept of Eurasia." *Current Anthropology* 57 (1): 1–26. https://doi.org/10.1086/684625.

Healey, Dan. 2001. *Homosexual Desires in Revolutionary Russia: The Regulation of Sexual and Gender Dissent*. Chicago: University of Chicago Press.

—. 2014. "From Stalinist Pariahs to Subjects of 'Managed Democracy': Queers in Moscow 1945 to the Present." In *Queer Cities, Queer Cultures: Europe Since 1945*, edited by Matt Cook and Jennifer V. Evans, 95–117. London: Bloomsbury.

Hemment, Julie. 2007. *Empowering Women in Russia: Activism, Aid, and NGOs.* Bloomington: Indiana University Press.

——. 2015. *Youth Politics in Putin's Russia: Producing Patriots and Entrepreneurs.* Bloomington: Indiana University Press.

Hirsch, Francine. 2005. *Empire of Nations: Ethnographic Knowledge and the Making of the Soviet Union.* Ithaca, NY: Cornell University Press.

Höjdestrand, Tova. 2009. *Needed by Nobody: Homelessness and Humanness in Post-Socialist Russia.* Ithaca, NY: Cornell University Press.

Humphrey, Caroline. 1983. *Karl Marx Collective: Economy, Society, and Religion in a Siberian Collective Farm.* Cambridge: Cambridge University Press.

——. 2002. "Does the category 'Postsocialist' still make sense?" In *Postsocialism: Ideals, Ideologies, and Practices in Eurasia,* edited by Chris Hann, 15–28. London: Routledge.

Jonson, Lena. 2015. *Art and Protest in Putin's Russia.* New York: Routledge.

Keck, Margaret, and Kathryn Sikkink. 1998. *Activists Beyond Borders: Advocacy Networks in International Politics.* Ithaca, NY: Cornell University Press.

Kelly, Catriona, Hilary Pilkington, David Shepherd, and Vadim Volkov. 1998. "Introduction: Why Cultural Studies?" In *Russian Cultural Studies: An Introduction,* edited by Catriona Kelly and David Shepherd, 1–21. Oxford: Oxford University Press.

Kon, Igor S. 1995. *The Sexual Revolution in Russia: From the Age of Czars to Today.* New York: Free Press.

Lapidus, Gail W. 1978. *Women in Soviet Society: Equality, Development, and Social Change.* Berkeley: University of California Press.

Ledeneva, Alena. 1998. *Russia's Economy of Favors: Blat, Networking, and Informal Exchange.* Cambridge: Cambridge University Press.

Lemon, Alaina. 2000. *Between Two Fires: Gypsy Performance and Romanian Memory from Pushkin to Post-Socialism.* Durham: Duke University Press. https://doi.org/10.1215/9780822381327.

Lomasko, Victoria. 2017. *Other Russias.* London: Penguin.

Mandel, Ruth. 2012. "Introduction: Transition to Where? Developing Post-Soviet Space." *Slavic Review* 71 (2): 223–33. https://doi.org/10.1017/S0037677900013590.

Markowitz, Fran. 1993. *A Community in Spite of Itself: Soviet Jewish Emigrés in New York.* Washington: Smithsonian Institution Press.

Marsch, Rosalind, ed. 1996. *Women in Russia and Ukraine.* Cambridge: Cambridge University Press.

Martin, Terry. 2001. *The Affirmative Action Empire: Nations and Nationalism in the Soviet Union, 1923–1939.* Ithaca, NY: Cornell University Press.

Mickiewicz, Ellen. 2014. *No Illusions: The Voices of Russia's Future Leaders.* Oxford: Oxford University Press. https://doi.org/10.1093/acprof:oso/9780199977833.001.0001.

Narayan, Kirin. 2012. *Alive in the Writing: Crafting Ethnography in the Company of Chekhov.* Chicago: University of Chicago Press. https://doi.org/10.7208/chicago/9780226567921.001.0001.

Navaro-Yashin, Yael. 2002. *Faces of the State: Secularism and Public Life in Turkey.* Princeton: Princeton University Press.

Nugent, David. 2008. "Democracy Otherwise: Struggles Over Popular Rule in the Northern Peruvian Andes." In *Democracy: Anthropological Approaches*, edited by Julia Paley, 21–62. Santa Fe, NM: School for Advanced Research Press.

Oates, Sarah. 2006. *Television, Democracy, and Elections in Russia*. London: Routledge.

Ortner, Sherry. 1996. *The Politics and Erotics of Culture*. Boston: Beacon Press.

Oushakine, Serguei. 2001. "The Terrifying Mimicry of *Samizdat*." *Public Culture*. 13 (2): 191–214.

—. 2009. *The Patriotism of Despair: Nation, War, and Loss in Russia*. Ithaca, NY: Cornell University Press.

Patico, Jennifer. 2008. *Consumption and Social Change in a Post-Soviet Middle Class*. Stanford: Stanford University Press.

Paxson, Margaret. 2005. *Solovyovo: The Story of Memory in a Russian Village*. Bloomington: Indiana University Press.

Pesmen, Dale. 2000. *Russia and Soul*. Ithaca, NY: Cornell University Press.

Petryna, Adriana. 2002. *Life Exposed: Biological Citizens after Chernobyl*. Princeton: Princeton University Press.

Pilkington, Hilary. 1998. *Migration, Displacement, and Identity in Post-Soviet Russia*. London: Routledge. https://doi.org/10.4324/9780203444436.

—, ed. 1996. *Gender, Generation, and Identity in Contemporary Russia*. New York: Routledge. https://doi.org/10.4324/9780203219089.

Reed-Danahay, Deborah, and Caroline Brettell, eds. 2008. *Citizenship, Political Engagement, and Belonging: Immigrants in Europe and the United States*. New Brunswick: Rutgers University Press.

Reeves, Madeleine. 2013. "Clean Fake: Authenticating Documents and Persons in Migrant Moscow." *American Ethnologist* 40 (3): 508–24.

Rethmann, Petra. 2016. "What Should Be Done? Art and Political Possibility in Russia." In *Impulse to Act: A New Anthropology of Resistance and Social Justice*, edited by Othon Alexandrakis, 152–79. Bloomington: Indiana University Press. https://doi.org/10.2307/j.ctt2005rdp.12.

—. 2008. "Nostalgie à Moscou." *Anthropologie et Sociétés* 32 (1–2): 85–102. https://doi.org/10.7202/018884ar.

—. 2004. "A Dream of Democracy in the Russian Far East." In *In the Way of Development: Indigenous Peoples, Life Projects, and Globalization*, edited by Glenn McRae, Mario Blaser, and Harvey Feit, 256–78. London: Zed Books.

—. 2001. *Tundra Passages: History and Gender in the Russian Far East*. University Park: Pennsylvania State University Press.

Ries, Nancy. 1997. *Russian Talk: Culture and Conversation during Perestroika*. Ithaca, NY: Cornell University Press.

—. 2002. "'Honest Bandits' and 'Warped People': Russian Narratives about Money, Corruption, and Moral Decay." In *Ethnography in Unstable Places*, edited by Carol Greenhouse, Elizabeth Mertz, and Kay Warren, 276–315. Durham: Duke University Press, 2002. https://doi.org/10.1215/9780822383482-010.

Rivkin-Fish, Michele. 2005. *Women's Health in Post-Soviet Russia: The Politics of Intervention*. Bloomington: Indiana University Press.

109

Rivkin-Fish, Michele, and Elena Trubina, eds. 2010. *Dilemmas of Diversity after the Cold War: Analyses of Cultural Difference*. Washington: Kennan Institute/Woodrow Wilson International Center for Scholars.

Roberman, Sveta. 2015. *Sweet Burdens: Welfare and Communality among Russian Jews in Germany*. New York: State University of New York Press.

Rogers, Douglas, 2009. *The Old Faith and the Russian Land: A Historical Ethnography of Ethics in the Urals*. Ithaca, NY: Cornell University Press.

—. 2015. *The Depths of Russia: Oil, Power, and Culture after Socialism*. Ithaca, NY: Cornell University Press.

Roudakova, Natalia. 2017. *Losing Pravda: Ethics, Truth, and Post-Truth Russia*. Cambridge: Cambridge University Press. https://doi.org/10.1017/9781316817117.

Schuler, Catherine. 2013. "Reinventing the Show Trial: Putin and Pussy Riot." *Drama Review* 57 (1): 7–17. https://doi.org/10.1162/DRAM_e_00230.

Scott, James. 1990. *Domination and the Arts of Resistance: Hidden Transcripts*. New Haven: Yale University Press.

Shekhovtsov, Anton. 2018. *Russia and the Western Right*. New York: Routledge.

Shevchenko, Olga. 2009. *Crisis and the Everyday in Postsocialist Moscow*. Bloomington: Indiana University Press.

—, ed. 2014. *Double Exposure: Memory and Photography*. London: Routledge.

Slezkine, Yuri. 1994. "The USSR as Communal Apartment, or How a Socialist State Promoted Ethnic Particularism." *Slavic Review* 53 (2): 414–52. https://doi.org/10.2307/2501300.

Smith, Kathleen. 2002. *Mythmaking in the New Russia: Politics and Memory in the Yeltsin Era*. Ithaca, NY: Cornell University Press.

Sokolovskiy, Sergey. 2011. "In a Zeitnot: Notes on the State of Russian Anthropology." *Laboratorium* (2): 70–89.

Sperling, Valerie. 2015. *Sex, Politics, and Putin*. Oxford: Oxford University Press.

Ssorin-Chaikov, Nikolai. 2003. *The Social Life of the State in Subarctic Siberia*. Stanford: Stanford University Press.

—. 2006. "On Heterochrony: Birthday Gifts to Stalin, 1949." *Journal of the Royal Anthropological Institute* 12 (2): 355–75. https://doi.org/10.1111/j.1467-9655.2006.00295.x.

—. 2013. "Ethnographic Conceptualism: An Introduction." *Laboratorium* 2 (13). Available on www.soclabo.org/index.php/laboratorium, accessed on July 28, 2017.

Stella, Francesca. 2013. "Queer Space, Pride, and Shame in Moscow." *Slavic Review* 72(3): 458–80. https://doi.org/10.5612/slavicreview.72.3.0458.

Stites, Richard. 1978. *The Women's Liberation Movement: Feminism, Nihilism, and Bolshevism, 1860–1930*. Princeton: Princeton University Press.

Stoler, Ann L. 2002. *Carnal Knowledge and Imperial Power: Race and the Intimate in Colonial Rule*. Durham: Duke University Press.

Suhr, Christian, and Rane Willerslev, eds. 2013. *Transcultural Montage*. New York: Berghahn.

Suny, Ronald. 1993. *The Revenge of the Past: Nationalism, Revolution, and the Collapse of the Soviet Union*. Stanford: Stanford University Press.

—. 2012. "The Contradictions of Identity: Being Soviet and National in the USSR and After." In *Soviet and Post-Soviet Identities*, edited by Mark Bassin and Catriona Kelly, 17–36. Cambridge: Cambridge University Press.

Taussig, Michael. 1986. *Shamanism, Colonialism, and the Wild Man: A Study in Terror and Healing*. Chicago: University of Chicago Press.

Temkina, Anna, and Anna Rotkirch. 1997. "Soviet Gender Contracts and their Shifts in Contemporary Russia." In *Russia in Transition: The Case of New Collective Actors and New Collective Actions*, edited by Anna Temkina, 195–203. Helsinki: Kikimora.

Trouillot, Michel-Rolph. 2004. *Global Transformations: Anthropology and the Modern World*. New York: Palgrave Macmillan.

Uehling, Greta L. 2004. *Beyond Memory: The Deportation and Return of the Crimean Tatars*. New York: Palgrave. https://doi.org/10.1057/9781403981271.

Utrata, Jennifer. 2015. *Women Without Men: Single Mothers and Family Change in the New Russia*. Ithaca, NY: Cornell University Press.

Venturi, Franco. 2001. *Roots of Revolution: A History of the Populist and Socialist Movements in 19th Century Russia*. London: Phoenix Press.

Wanner, Catherine. 1998. *Burden of Dreams: History and Identity in Post-Soviet Ukraine*. University Park, PA: The Pennsylvania State University Press.

Weber, Max. 1958. *From Max Weber: Essays in Sociology*. Oxford: Oxford University Press.

Wedel, Janine. 1998. *Collision and Collusion: The Strange Case of Western Aid to Eastern Europe, 1989–1998*. New York: St. Martin's Press.

Williams, Raymond. 1977. *Marxism and Literature*. Oxford: Oxford University Press.

Wolfe, Thomas. 2005. *Soviet Journalism: The Press and the Socialist Person after Stalin*. Bloomington: Indiana University Press.

Wood, Elizabeth. 1997. *The Baba and the Comrade: Gender and Politics in Revolutionary Russia*. Bloomington: Indiana University Press.

Yurchak, Alexei. 2003. "Russian Neoliberal: The Entrepreneurial Ethic and the Spirit of 'True Careerism.'" *Russian Review* 62 (1): 72–90. https://doi.org/10.1111/1467-9434.00264.

—. 2006. *Everything Was Forever, Until It Was No More: The Last Soviet Generation*. Princeton: Princeton University Press.

—. 2008a. "Necro-Utopia: The Politics of Indistinction and the Art of the Non-Soviet." *Current Anthropology* 49 (2): 199–224. https://doi.org/10.1086/526098.

—. 2008b. "Post-Post Soviet Sincerity: Young Pioneers, Cosmonauts, and Other Soviet Heroes Born Today." In *What is Soviet Now?*, edited by Thomas Lahusen and Peter Solomon, 257–76. Münster: Lit Verlag.

Zigon, Jarrett. 2011. *"HIV Is God's Blessing": Rehabilitating Morality in Neoliberal Russia*. Berkeley: University of California Press.

111

INDEX

A

abortion, 67–68
Abuladze, Tengiz, 11
Academy of Sciences, 4
activism
    and art, 82–84
    of Chukchi people, 42, 43
    history of, 54–59
    against homophobia, 69, 70–71
    preparations, 57
    Pussy Riot, 47–48, 53–54
    against Putin, 47, 50, 55, 56
    self-publishing, 78–80
Afghanistan, 9, 11, 76
agency, 101
aktions. See activism
alcohol, 67
Alternative for Germany (AfD), 89, 92,
    93, 94
Anadyr, 43–44
Anderson, Benedict, 36
Andropov, Yuri, 9
anthropology, 1–3, 5–6, 15, 41–42, 52
anti-Semitism, 26
Appadurai, Arjun, 7
applied anthropology, 41
Armenians, 12
art, 80–84, 101
Ashwin, Sarah, 63
Association of Sexual Minorities (ASM),
    70–71
authoritarianism. *See* Putin, Vladimir;
    Stalin, Joseph; Stalinism
avant-garde, 80, 82, 85, 101
Azerbaijan, 12
Azhgikhina, Nadezhda, 73

B

baba, 63
Bakhtin, Mikhail, 38
Bernstein, Anya, 31–32, 50–51

bespredel, 14–15
black market, 7
blat', 14, 17, 101
Bloch, Alexia, 89–90
"Blue Buckets," 82
Bogoraz, Vladimir, 4
Bolotnaya Square, 56
Bolshevik Revolution, 8
bomzhi, 18–19
book usage, 5–6
Borysenko, Veronika, 91
Bourdieu, Pierre, 16
Boym, Svetlana, 24
Brammer, Mascha, 91
Brezhnev, Leonid, 9
Brown, Kate, 11, 43
Brown, Wendy, 52
Brubaker, Rogers, 36, 40–41
Buddhism, 31–32
Burnt by the Sun (film), 80
Buryatia farm, 10
Butler, Judith, 64, 65

C

Caldwell, Melissa, 2
cancer, 13
capitalism, 8, 10–11, 15, 16–17
    See also neoliberalism
Catherine the Great, 94
centralization, 17
Chaadaev, Petr, 39
Chechnya, 22–23, 74
Cheka, 8
Chekhov, Anton, 2
Chernenko, Konstantin, 9
Chernobyl disaster, 12–13
chernukha, 15, 81
Chirikova, Yevgenia, 55–56
chöd, 31
Christian Democratic Union (CDU), 97
chto delat' collective, 78–80, 79, 81–82

Chukchi people, 42–45
Chukotka National District, 43–44
city planning, 11
civil society, 101
Cold War, 11–12, 101
collective memory, 22, 101
collectives, 35–36, 39, 78–80, 83–85
    See also kolkhoz system
Collier, Stephen, 11
Committee for State Security (KGB), 9
commodities, 16–17, 101
Commonwealth of Independent States
    (CIS), 12
communities, 35–36
conformity, 84–85
conservatism, 97
conspicuous consumption, 16–17, 101
constructivism, 101
Consumption and Change in a Post-Soviet
    Middle Class (Patico), 16
"core nation," 36
corporal punishment, 51
corruption
    blue car lights, 82
    elections, 49, 50, 52
    of "new Russians," 18
    protest against, 56
cosmology, 101
coup d'état, 12, 14
Crown of Monomakh, 82
culture
    changes, 7–8
    cosmology collapse, 21
    definition, 101
    and fashion, 16
    and meaning, 3, 4
    overview, 1–5
    and peasants, 4
    political, 48–51
    as porous, 16
    ritualization, 41
    and Soviet Union, 4–5, 10
    and Stalinism, 4–5
    undermining bureaucracy, 10
currency exchange, 7
cynicism, 55, 77–78, 80
Czechoslovakia, 9

D
debts, 14
democracy, 48, 51–53, 101
The Depths of Russia (Rogers), 50

diaspora, 89, 102
disorder, 15
dissidents, 9, 30, 55, 102
    See also activism
diversity, 2
    See also multinationalism
drug users, 31
Dugin, Aleksandr, 91
dusha, 38–39
Dzhugashvili, Iosif Vissarionovich. *See*
    Stalin, Joseph

E
Eichhorn, Jonas, 91
emic approaches, 29, 102
empathy wall, 89
Engels, Friedrich, 9
Enlightenment, 4, 39, 102
entrepreneurship, 39, 81
    See also small business
essentialism, 3, 102
ethnicity, 37–38
ethnographic close-ups
    activism, 47–48, 57, 83–84
    art, 83–85
    black market currency
        exchange, 7
    gender, 61–62
    immigration, 93
    journalism, 78–80
    nostalgia, *27, 28*
ethnographic studies
    after Soviet Union collapse, 35
    in book, 1, 5
    early, 4
    of queer sexuality, 71
    of women's health care, 68
ethnography, definition, 102
Eurasian Youth Movement, 91
Eurasianism, 90–91, 102
everyday culture, 3
exile, 9

F
Faraday, George, 80, 81
farms, collective, 9, 10, 31
fashion, 16, *26, 27*
Federal Security Services (FSB),
    83–84
feminism, 63, 69–70
    See also gender relations; women
fieldwork, 1, 102

film, 55, 80–81
    See also individual films
First Chechen War, 21, 23
folk culture, 3
Foucault, Michel, 53, 64

G

Gabowitsch, Mischa, 58
Geertz, Clifford, 58
Gellner, Ernest, 37
gender, 62–63, 64–70, 102
    See also feminism; masculinity;
        women
Germany, 89, 92–98
glamur, 81–82
glasnost, 11, 12, 29, 76
globalization, 15, 102
gold market, *18*
Gorbachev, Mikhail
    assuming power, 11
    and Chernobyl, 13
    and news bridges, 76
    resigning, 12
    and Russian Germans, 95
    on women, 66
Goscilo, Helena, 81–82
governmentality, 53, 102
Grant, Bruce, 2, 4, 25
grants, 52
Gray, Patty, 43
Great Terror, 25–26, 28, 80–81
GULAG, 25–26, 28, 70
The Gulag Archipelago (Solzhenitsyn), 11
Gumilev, Lev Nikolaevich, 38
Gusinsky, Vladimir, 76

H

Halbwachs, Maurice, 22
hammer and sickle, 8
Healey, Dan, 69–70
hegemonic masculinity, 102
Helsinki Accords, 9
Hemment, Julie, 36, 39, 52, 53
high culture, 3
Hochschild, Arlie, 89
Hofer, Johannes, 24
Höjdestrand, Tova, 18–19
home, as feeling, 94
homelessness, 18–19
homophobia, 47, 63, 65, 69–70
Humphrey, Caroline, 10, 18
Hungary, 9

I

identity, 35–39, 40, 64–66, 90–91, 102
ideology, 10, 102
Imagined Communities (Anderson), 36
immigration, 92–93, 94, 95–98
    See also migration
indigenization, 41
Indigenous Peoples, 2, 4, 39–45
industrialization, 8–9
inequality, 18
inflation, 13
innocence, 25, 28–29
Institute of the Peoples of the North, 4
instrumental rationality, 9–10
intelligentsia, 4, 102
International Day of Indigenous Peoples,
    43–44
International Monetary Fund (IMF),
    13–14
International Women's Day, 61
internet, 2, 3, 53, 77
    See also media
Internews, 73
Ionto (Indigenous Person), 42, 43

J

Jonson, Lena, 74
journalism, 56, 73–74, 76–80
    See also media

K

Kamchatka, 7, 87–88
Karl, Marx, 9
Kasparov, Garry, 55
Keck, Margaret, 88–89
KGB (Committee for State Security), 9
Khimki Forest Protests, 55–56
Khodorovsky, Mikhail, 49
Khrushchev, Nikita, 9
knouts, 51
Kohl, Helmut, 95
kolkhoz system, 9, 10, 31
Konstantin Palace, 81–82
kulaks, 9

L

labor camps, 25–26, 28, 70
Lapidus, Gail, 65–66
Lavrov, Sergei, 93
Law on Individual Economic Activity, 11
Law on Public Gatherings, 54
Lenin, Vladimir, 8

115

LGBTQ people, 69–71, 82–83
   See also homophobia
life stories, 13, 21–22, 103
Lisa F., 93–94
Lomasko, Victoria, 83
loss
   definition, 103
   and pensions, 23
   and Russian ethnicity, 37
   and Soviet Union collapse, 21
   "way of life," 24, 81

M

Mamyshev-Monroe, Vladik, 65
Manezh Square, 7
Marches of the Dissenters, 55
Martin, Terry, 40–41, 43
masculinity, 62–63, 67, 102
mass culture, 3
meaning
   and culture, 3, 4
   definition, 101, 103
   monuments, 25
   search for, 21–23, 36
means of production, 103
media, 2, 3, 73–74, 75–80, 103
   See also film; internet; journalism;
      television shows
media blackout, 13
Medvedev, Dmitry, 56, 84
Memorial, 25–26, 30
memory, 22, 23–24, 25–30, 42–43
men and gender roles, 67
Merkel, Angela, 97–98
methodology, 1–2
Meuthen, Jörg, 92
migration, 87–98, 103
   See also immigration
Mikhalkov, Nikita, 80–81
Miklukho-Maklai, Nikolai, 4
military costumes, *26*
montage, 80
monuments, 25
morality, 68–69
Moscow Doesn't Believe in Tears (film), 81
multinationalism, 2, 37–38, 40–41, 43
music, 16, 55
muzhik, 63, 67

N

Narayan, Kirin, 2
nationalism, 26, 36–37, 38–39, 41, 103
nations, definitions, 36, 103
Navalny, Alexei, 56, 77
   See also activism
Nazarov, Aleksandr, 43, 45
Nemtsov, Boris, 49
neoliberalism, 17, 47, 69, 103
NGOs (nongovernmental organizations),
   53, 54
Nicholas II (Tsar), 8
nostalgia, 24, *27*, 28–29, 81, 103
nuclear power, 12–13

O

ocherk, 75
oil industry, 49–50
Old Believers, 30–31
oligarchs, 14, 103
online media, 2, 3
   See also internet; journalism; media
Oushakine, Serguei, 21, 29, 38

P

Pamiat, 26
participant observation, 1, 103
Patico, Jennifer, 16
Patriarch Kirill of Moscow, 47
The Patriotism of Despair (Oushakine), 21
Pavlenskii, Petr, 83
Paxson, Margaret, 15, 29
peasants
   Bolshevism, 8
   and culture, 4
   in film, 81
   kulaks, 9
   and land, 11
   and workers, 63
perestroika, 11, 13, 25, 95, 103
performativity, 64–65, 83–85, 103
Perm, 50
Pesmen, Dale, 38
Peter the Great (Tsar), 4, 25, 39
Petryna, Adriana, 12, 13
Philosophical Letters (Chaadaev), 39
Plamber, Jan, 29
Pokaianie (film), 11
Politkovskaya, Anna, 74, 78
post-socialism, 17–18, 23, 24, 103
poverty, 13, 18–19
power, 50–51, 64
"practical realism," 69
Prague Spring, 9
Prigov, Dmitri, 84

116

"Prisoner of the Caucasus" (Pushkin), 2
privatization, 66–67, 76
public spheres, 53–54, 103
Pushkin, Aleksandr, 2
Pussy Riot, 47–48, 50, 53–54, 83
Putin, Vladimir
    cynicism, 78
    elections of, 17, 50
    history of government, 49–50
    and Politkovskaya, 74, 78
    protest against, 47, 50, 55, 56
    as Pussy Riot target, 47
the putsch, 12

Q

queer, word usage, 64
queer people. *See* LGBTQ people

R

rakushki, 15
Red Army, 8
Reeves, Madeleine, 88
refugees, 92, 96, 97–98
religion, 22, 30–32, 68, 103
repression
    Great Terror, 25–26, 28, 80–81
    of journalism, 73–74
    Law on Public Gatherings, 54
    of opposition leader, 50
    of protestors, 56–57
    sexual, 70
    show trails, 48
Revolt of the Filmmakers (Faraday), 80–81
Ries, Nancy, 13
rituals
    activism, 58
    chöd, 31–32
    Chukotka recognition, 44–45
    culture, 41
    elections, 58
    life stories, 13
    Sepych Old Believers, 31
    speeches, 10, 13
    war, 22
Rivkin-Fish, Michele, 2, 18, 68–69
Rogers, Douglas, 30–31, 50
Roudakova, Natalia, 75, 77
Russia and Soul (Pesmen), 38
Russian Association of the Indigenous
    Peoples of the North (RAIPON), 41
Russian ethnicity, 37–38
Russian Federation

and identity, 37
and migration, 87–88
size of, 2
and Soviet past, 25
Russian Geographical Society, 4
Russian Germans, 89, 92–98
Russian Orthodox Church (ROC), 31
    See also religion
russkii mir, 90–91, 103–104
Rutskoi, Aleksandr, 14

S

samizdat, 75, 104
Scott, James, 54
"Secret Speech," 9
self-publishing, 78–80, 79
Sepych, 30–31
sexuality. *See* homophobia; LGBTQ people
Shevchenko, Olga, 15
shock therapy, 14
Siberia, 10
Sikkink, Kathryn, 88–89
Sinie nosy, 82–83
Slavophiles, 39
small business, 8, 11
    See also entrepreneurship
social movements, 54–55
    See also activism
socialism
    vs. capitalism, 10–11
    definition, 9–10, 104
    history of, 8–9
    hypernormalized, 10
    mourning loss of, 24
    transition from, 14–15, 25
Soeder, Markus, 93
Sokolovskiy, Sergey, 2
Solzhenitsyn, Aleksandr, 11
sots-art, 82, 104
soul, 38–39
souvenirs, 28–29
sovereignty, 49, 50–51, 104
Soviet Union
    and Cold War end, 12
    collapse, 12, 13, 21, 22, 35
    creation of, 8
    and culture, 4–5, 10
    definition, 104
    and gender, 65–66
    key aims, 41
    and ritualized speeches, 10, 13
    and Russians, 37

speeches, 10
Sperling, Valerie, 62
Ssorin-Chaikov, Nikolai, 10
stability, 15, 17, 25
Stalin, Joseph
    cult of personality,
        28–29, 80
    and experiments, 54
    modernizing economy, 8–9
    nostalgia for, *27*, 28–29
    overview, 27–28
    and Russian Germans, 95
Stalinism
    and culture, 4–5
    definition, 104
    memorials, 25–26
    overview, 27–28
    trials, 48
state, definition, 104
state power, 48–49
state rhetoric, 10, 13
stiob, 82, 104
Stites, Richard, 54
Strukov, Vald, 81–82

T
Taussig, Michael, 80
television, 16, 76–77
    See also media
Theater Square, 57–58
theater-states, 58
totalitarianism, 10, 24, 104
trade activism, 42
trade fairs, 42–43
the transition, 14–15, 25, 104
transnational advocacy networks
    (TANs), 88–89
transnationalism, 88–89,
    90–91, 104
Trubina, Elena, 2
Tsereteli, Zurab, 25
Turkey, 89–90
Tver', 52–53
Tynel', Anton, 42, 43

U
Ukraine, 12–13, 90–91
Ukrainians, 87–88, 90–91
Uminskii, Gennadi, 21, 23
Union of Soviet Socialist
    Republics (USSR).
    See Soviet Union
Utrata, Jennifer, 68–69

V
veterans, 23
voina collective, 83–85
Volga German Autonomous Socialist
    Republic, 95
Vysotskii, Vladimir, 55
Vzgliad news agency, 76

W
wages, 17
wars
    Afghanistan, 9, 11, 76
    Chechnya, 21, 22–23
    Cold War, 11–12, 101
    World War II, 29, 30, 95
wealth, 18
Weber, Max, 50
Wedel, Janine, 52
the West, definition, 104
Western influences
    capitalism, 11, 15, 52
    democracy, 52–53
    funding anthropology research, 2–3
    individualism, 39
    media, 16, 55, 81
Westernizers, 39
White Army, 8
Williams, Raymond, 94
Wolfe, Thomas, 75–76
women
    chöd, 31–32
    domestic violence, 52–53
    gender roles, 61–63, 65–66
    and *knouts*, 51
    migration, 89–90
    and privatization, 66–67
    and reproductive health, 67–69
    sexual discrimination, 69–70
    in Soviet era, 65–66
Wood, Elizabeth, 63
World Bank, 13–14
World War II, 29, 30, 95

Y
Yeltsin, Boris, 12, 14, 22–23
Young Pioneers, *27*
youth, 36–37, 39
Yurchak, Alexei, 10, 16, 54–55, 75, 80

Z
Zhenskii Svet, 52–53
Zigon, Jarret, 31
zines, 78–80, *79*

118